Engaging Russia as Partner and Participant

The Next Stage of NATO–Russia Relations

Robert E. Hunter, Sergey M. Rogov

Supported by the Carnegie Corporation of New York, the RAND Corporation, and the Foundation for East-West Bridges of Moscow

RAND NATIONAL SECURITY RESEARCH DIVISION

The work described here was supported by the Carnegie Corporation of New York, the RAND Corporation, and the Foundation for East-West Bridges of Moscow.

ISBN 0-8330-3705-6

The RAND Corporation is a nonprofit research organization providing objective analysis and effective solutions that address the challenges facing the public and private sectors around the world. RAND's publications do not necessarily reflect the opinions of its research clients and sponsors.

RAND® is a registered trademark.

Published 2004 by the RAND Corporation
1776 Main Street, P.O. Box 2138, Santa Monica, CA 90407-2138
1200 South Hayes Street, Arlington, VA 22202-5050
201 North Craig Street, Suite 202, Pittsburgh, PA 15213-1516
RAND URL: http://www.rand.org/
To order RAND documents or to obtain additional information, contact
Distribution Services: Telephone: (310) 451-7002;
Fax: (310) 451-6915; Email: order@rand.org

Preface

In late 2001, the RAND Corporation joined with the Institute for the USA and Canadian Studies of the Russian Academy of Sciences (ISKRAN) to investigate the possibilities of developing cooperation between the North Atlantic Treaty Organization (NATO) and Russia. The cochairmen of the Working Group on NATO-Russia Relations, Ambassador Robert Hunter, Senior Advisor, RAND, and Dr. Sergey Rogov, Director, ISKRAN, recruited a group of 31 senior American and Russian experts and practitioners, including academics, former diplomats and policymakers, and retired flag officers. The report of the working group was published in April 2002 and presented to key governments and personally to the Secretary-General of NATO, Lord Robertson.[1]

That report surveyed the work of the Permanent Joint Council that the NATO-Russia Founding Act of 1997 had created and looked toward the impending creation of a new NATO-Russia Council. The report was designed in part to help in the design of the new council; some of its recommendations remain apposite.

A year later, in part because of encouragement from various government and NATO officials, RAND and ISKRAN decided to reconvene the Working Group on NATO-Russian Relations, again under the joint chairmanship of Messrs. Hunter and Rogov. This time, in addition to U.S. and Russian participants, the working group has also included participants from Canada and Europe, reflecting the judgment that NATO-Russia relations cannot be developed just by the United States and Russia but must involve NATO's Canadian and European members. We were also fortunate, once again, to have the generous support of Carnegie Corporation of New York which, along with the RAND Corporation and the Foundation for East-West Bridges of Moscow, made this project possible.

The current report is the collective product of the 42 U.S., Russian, Canadian, and European members of the working group. The views expressed in this report are those of the participants in their own personal capacities, not necessarily those of RAND, ISKRAN, or the other organizations with which panel members are affiliated. Not every participant necessarily agrees with all of report's conclusions, but—as with the earlier report—the cochairmen are gratified that the degree of common judgment has proven to be so high. As with the earlier report, there are—remarkably—no formal dissenting views.

During the course of its deliberations and other work between April 2003 and May 2004, the working group met in six formal and informal sessions: twice in Moscow (June 30–July 1, 2003 and March 14–16, 2004), once in Brussels (October 17–19, 2003), and

---

[1] Robert E. Hunter, Sergey M. Rogov, and Olga Oliker, "NATO and Russia: Bridge-Building for the 21st Century," Santa Monica, Calif.: RAND Corporation, WP-128-NSRD/RC, April 2002; online at http://www.rand.org/publications/WP/WP128/ (as of 22 September 2004).

twice at RAND's offices in Arlington, Virginia, with project members conducting further explorations in Brussels (March 4–5, 2004). We were fortunate, at the first Moscow meeting, to have the participation of Rolf Welberts, Director of NATO's Information Office in Moscow and, in Brussels, of a number of NATO officials, including Jean Fournet, Assistant Secretary General for Public Diplomacy, and Paul Fritch, Head of Section, Russia and Ukraine Relations. We are deeply grateful to all of them. These meetings were instrumental in guiding the working group's deliberations, especially in helping to ensure that we did not simply "reinvent the wheel."

The report that follows is neither an analysis of the work that the NATO-Russia Council has been doing since its creation nearly two years ago nor a compendium of NATO-Russia cooperation, actual or possible. Instead, it seeks to single out a few particularly important areas in which cooperation could be enhanced. These are centered around three subjects: the completion of the 20th century security agenda in Europe; the opening of the 21st century security agenda beyond Europe (especially as defined functionally by terrorism and weapons of mass destruction and geographically as the region between the Mediterranean and Central Asia); and the (unresolved) issue of the long-term future of Russia's relationship *with*, and potentially *within* NATO. It is thus hoped that this report can help to illuminate choices and possibilities for NATO and Russia in their relations with one another in the time following the NATO Istanbul Summit of June 2004. It is this long-term perspective that has motivated and shaped the presentation that follows.

Contents

Preface iii
Executive Summary vii

CHAPTER ONE
Introduction 1

CHAPTER TWO
NATO-Russia in Europe 6
Personnel Engagement, Exchanges, and Staffing 6
Military-to-Military Cooperation 8
Transformation, Interoperability, and Defense Industrial Relations 10
Civil Emergencies 12
Arms Control: The Treaty on Conventional Armed Forces in Europe 13

CHAPTER THREE
NATO-Russia Beyond Europe 16
The Political and Geopolitical Context 16
A Russian Role with NATO on Afghanistan 18
A Russian Role in Iraq 20
Cooperation in Central Asia and the Transcaucasus 21
Israeli-Palestinian Peacekeeping 23
New Middle East Security System 23

CHAPTER FOUR
The Future of Russia *Within* NATO 25

APPENDIX A
RAND-ISKRAN Working Group on NATO-Russia Relations 29

APPENDIX B
The NATO-Russia Dialogue: An (Unrepentantly) European View
Alyson J. K. Bailes 31

APPENDIX C
NATO-Russia Military Cooperation
Dieter Farwick 37

APPENDIX D

Prospects for Elaboration of Joint Doctrines of Peacemaking Activities of Russia and NATO: Russia's Possible Role in NATO Rapid Reaction Forces

U. V. Morozov 41

APPENDIX E

Outlook for Cooperation Between the Defense and Industrial Complexes of Russia and the NATO Countries

Vladimir Rubanov 51

APPENDIX F

Political Relations: RUSSIA, NATO, and the European Union

Vitaliy Zhurkin 67

Executive Summary

In May 1997, NATO concluded a Founding Act with the Russian Federation.[1] Then, following the September 11, 2001, terrorist attacks in the United States, NATO and the Russian Federation agreed to create a NATO-Russia Council (NRC), "where NATO member states and Russia will work *as equal partners* in areas of common interest."[2]

This report does not review in detail the record of the NATO-Russia Council. Rather, it points to some additional areas in which the members of the NATO-Russia Working Group believe the NRC can usefully become engaged.

Whether the time has arrived for redefining Russia's relations with NATO—or *within* NATO—is the key point of this report. This matter has two dimensions: the fulfillment of a 20th-century security agenda to ensure that the last century's European tragedy will "never again" be visited and a new agenda for the 21st century, typified by three concerns: terrorism, the spread of weapons of mass destruction, and security for the broader Middle East. These two agendas include

- Russia's greater and more-integrated participation in security, political, economic, and other arrangements for the great ongoing experiment in determining future security in Europe and beyond
- Russia's role in the development of Western policy and practice in areas beyond Europe, especially in the Middle East, Central Asia, and the Transcaucasus.

In short, the next phase of NATO-Russia relations should focus on Russia's *greater engagement as a partner and a participant.*

NATO-Russia in Europe

The first task in forging this new NATO-Russian relationship has focused on what is possible and desirable within Europe. The NATO-Russia Working Group judges that a few key areas should be emphasized.

---

[1] The term *founding act* was chosen to avoid implying that the arrangements being negotiated had the effect of a treaty, which would have made it subject to ratification by the U.S. Senate and, potentially, by other NATO parliaments (U.S. request) but also to imply both the significance of the arrangements—*founding*—and that they had political if not also legal effect—*act* (Russian request).

[2] Founding Act on Mutual Relations, Cooperation and Security Between NATO and The Russian Federation, Paris, May 27, 1997; online at http://www.nato.int/docu/basictxt/fndact-a.htm (as of 22 September 2004).

Personnel Engagement, Exchanges, and Staffing

An important element of developing NATO-Russia relations is for Russian and NATO officials, personnel, and staffs to engage one another functionally. Much is being done. The following are some of the key areas needing further development:

- Engagement of top-level Russian diplomatic personnel in Brussels and at the key NATO commands and of top-level NATO diplomatic personnel with institutions in Russia, including the Foreign Ministry, should increase.
- Engagement of Russian and allied military personnel should increase in their respective headquarters (as well as in NATO-Brussels and the Russian Defense Ministry), including joint staff training and development of common and compatible doctrines, extending to such newer command structures as the NATO Response Force (NRF).
- Increasingly, the basic approach should be that *inclusion* is the rule and *exclusion* is the exception. NATO and Russia must increasingly seek counsel with one another in any crisis either faces.
- With agreement of the European Union (EU), Russian civilian and military observers should be included in NATO's work with the EU, including the Common Foreign and Security Policy (CFSP) and the European Security and Defense Policy (ESDP).

Military-to-Military Cooperation

The following are the key areas for development of military cooperation:

- Russian military planners should be consulted and engaged in developing NATO peacekeeping doctrine, including the NRF employment doctrine.
- Russia should create significant officer and enlisted training opportunities for NATO personnel in Russia, to parallel increased Russian participation in NATO and NATO-related schools.
- Russia should have a greater role in the Partnership Coordination Cell.
- Russia and other Euro-Atlantic Partnership Council (EAPC) states should be progressively engaged with NATO's Combined Joint Task Force (CJTF) headquarters. NATO and Russia should consider whether Russia should play a lead nation role in an NRF rotation.

Transformation, Interoperability, and Defense Industrial Relations

Acquainting Russian forces with NATO's common procedures will help these forces work effectively *with* and *within* NATO and help them develop habits of mind and behavior that can have positive political effects. Russia also needs to increase the interoperability of its forces, equipment, and techniques with NATO's. Key areas for development include the following:

- NATO has opened up some NATO standardization agreements (STANAGS) to Russia, which has adopted some of them. More will be needed. The West needs to address the problem of releasing higher technology data to Russia; Russia needs to show it can be trusted not to pass the data on to third parties.
- Russia should be more fully associated NATO's Conference of National Armaments Directors (CNAD). It should become associated with the NATO Defence Capabilities Commitment and become eligible to compete in providing a wide range of

equipment, including modernization of Soviet-made weapons in the armed forces of the new Alliance members.

- Russia should be progressively associated with NATO transformation, including work at Allied Command Transformation, consistent with security requirements. Here again, the goal should be *inclusion* as the norm and *exclusion* the exception.

- Russia should share its transformation work with NATO, engage NATO with its development, again working toward *inclusion* as the norm and *exclusion* the exception.

- Russia should take part in more NATO military exercises and peacekeeping.

Civil Emergencies

For nearly a decade, NATO and Russia have cooperated in civil emergency preparedness. NATO-Russia cooperation should be extended, in several areas:

- common staffing of headquarters and planning work
- developing joint doctrine
- combining relevant capabilities
- sharing intelligence
- conducting exercises
- deploying jointly to natural disasters (and potentially to sites of terrorist attacks).

Arms Control: The Treaty on Conventional Armed Forces in Europe

Disagreements over the Treaty on Conventional Armed Forces in Europe (CFE) need to be resolved promptly, with each side addressing the other's concerns.

For Russia, this would involve arrangements for relocating relatively small numbers of troops and amounts of equipment from Moldova and agreeing on the time frame and modalities for the withdrawal of Russian forces and equipment from Georgia. For NATO, accession to the treaty of the four non-CFE allies would codify existing political assurances of restraint in deploying forces closer to Russia's borders.

NATO member states should consider expanding financial assistance for the withdrawal process. Other efforts could include an NRC peacekeeping mission in Moldova to monitor a constitutional settlement.

NATO-Russia Beyond Europe

The events of September 11, 2001, and the 2003 War in Iraq changed much for NATO and NATO-Russian relations. A natural agenda has emerged in terms of key issues of terrorism and weapons of mass destruction (WMD). Regarding Russia's role, the Working Group believes the following:

- NATO's engagement in Asian territories bordering on Russia is not detrimental to Russia's security interests, and there is an urgent need for NATO-Russian cooperation and, potentially, even for joint action in and around these territories.

- Concerns and possibilities about Afghanistan, Iraq, and other parts of the Middle East should involve discussion and agreement (especially in the NATO-Russia Council) and practical steps in political, security, and military cooperation.

A Russian Role with NATO on Afghanistan

NATO's leadership of the UN-mandated International Security Assistance Force (ISAF) mission in Afghanistan presents an opportunity for NATO-Russia cooperation. The NRC should consider engaging Russia with ISAF, primarily outside Afghanistan, to

- monitor Afghanistan's borders
- combat drug trafficking and terrorism
- assist in the return of refugees to Afghanistan
- contribute to intelligence collection, assessment, and coordination
- help train and equip Afghanistan's police and armed forces
- assist in general reconstruction efforts.

Special command-and-control arrangements for Russian forces would be needed (perhaps using the Deputy to the Supreme Allied Commander, Europe, for Russian Forces, whom Russia should appoint), along with guiding principles for the Russian area of responsibility and military tasks in antidrug and antiterrorist operations. Whether there is strong resistance to Russian participation because of the Soviet Union's invasion in the 1980s may depend on the ability of NATO and Russia to reassure the Afghans that Russian participation does not pose a threat.

A Russian Role in Iraq

The period following the transition from the U.S.-led Coalition Provisional Authority to a sovereign Iraqi government might present an opportunity for NATO-Russian cooperation, depending on the desires of the Iraqi interim government.

NATO and Russia should consider participating in a joint civil-military operation in Iraq in 2005. This could take the form of special units in which NATO and Russia work together. Joint operational objectives could include the following:

- assisting in the monitoring of Iraq's borders
- improving the effectiveness of the National Police, army, and other security forces
- assisting the United Nations (UN), if present, with force protection and intelligence
- taking part in reconstruction efforts.

NATO and Russia would need to do the following:

- develop special command-and-control arrangement for Russian forces (perhaps using the Deputy to the Supreme Allied Commander, Europe, for Russian Forces)
- agree on guiding principles for NATO and Russian peacekeeping operations
- identify the Russian sectors of responsibility (or joint responsibility)
- outline the fundamental military tasks for Russian forces
- establish a legal framework acceptable to all parties.

Russia will never put its forces under NATO's military command, at least as long as it is not a full participant in allied political decisionmaking. Thus, Russia's military engagement in Iraq is unlikely, unless command arrangements were worked out through the NRC. Still, Iraq should be a central topic for consideration within the NATO-Russia Council, including political discussion, strategic assessments, coordination of policy, and appropriate activities regarding possible cooperation in Iraq.

Cooperation in Central Asia and the Transcaucasus

Central Asia and the Transcaucasus are areas for potential NATO-Russian cooperation, in the contexts both of the NRC and the Euro-Atlantic Partnership Council. NATO and Russia might conduct joint peacekeeping missions, preferably under a UN mandate. They might form a joint peacekeeping unit to monitor a (future) settlement of the Nagorno-Karabakh conflict or to conduct joint border protection in Tajikistan or Georgia.

NATO and Russia, along with states in the region, could also conduct joint exercises to combat terrorism in Central Asia, within the framework of the Partnership for Peace (PFP) or NRF. Technical obstacles can be surmounted, including language; financing (NATO countries should be ready to help underwrite these activities); and a Status of Forces Agreement.

Israeli-Palestinian Peacekeeping

In April 2003, the United States, Russia, the UN, and the EU published their "road map" for peacemaking between Israel and a prospective Palestinian state. The chances of success are problematical, but, at some point, peace negotiations may succeed and produce a two-state solution. Outside help will be needed to help preserve security and build confidence between the parties, perhaps a peacekeeping or "peace enabling" force, led by the United States and including NATO and Russian forces.

The Working Group on NATO-Russia Relations recommends that the NRC and military bodies begin considering such a development and its practical requirements.

New Middle East Security System

It is increasingly clear that a new "security system" is needed for the Middle East, especially for the Persian Gulf region. The West and Russia would benefit from a system among regional states that reduced the need for outside military engagement.

It would be useful for regional countries, NATO, and Russia to begin exploring a new structure and organization (modeled after the Organization for Security and Cooperation in Europe [OSCE] or another such organization, formal or informal, limited or comprehensive), developed on an inclusive, nondiscriminatory basis.

The Future of Russia *Within* NATO

The long-term nature of the NATO-Russia relationship requires a clear vision and a common strategy. The Founding Act and the new NATO-Russia Council have helped, but they still do not point to a lasting solution.

One school of thought has argued that Russia would be unlikely ever to join NATO. Another school has argued that, nevertheless, the notion of "equal opportunity" to join should be preserved. A third school has suggested some form of "associate" membership. A final school foresees relatively near-term full membership. In the West, the last view has been restricted largely to a limited group of people who see the Alliance as a second OSCE. In

Russia, proponents generally want NATO to become a political and security association instead of a military alliance.

The Working Group on NATO-Russia relations believes it is time to revisit the question of Russia's long-term engagement with NATO. This is not a recommendation for Russia today to seek or be accorded NATO membership. It is about developing the idea of a deeply engaged role for Russia in deliberations about the future of areas contiguous to it, as well as about "globalization."

The objectives in NATO-Russia relations should be to

- solidify the practical bases for day-to-day NATO-Russia cooperation
- work toward a true sense of "equality" in NATO-Russia activities
- ensure that what they do together preserves the interests of third parties
- build confidence, at all levels, and progressively look toward common actions
- promote Russian-EU cooperation
- intensify personnel exchanges and educational opportunities
- promote complementarity and cooperation of nonofficial relationships, including the private sector and nongovernmental organizations.

At heart, the NATO-Russia relationship will be about what NATO and Russia do together to develop a truly equal, mutually supportive relationship that promotes the goal of a "Europe whole and free"—and beyond. NATO and Russia should share responsibilities, and each should behave responsibly toward the other.

CHAPTER ONE

Introduction

For several decades, the Soviet Union and the North Atlantic Treaty Organization (NATO) were engaged in a dangerous confrontation. The end of the Cold War, the collapse of the Warsaw Pact, and the dissolution of the Soviet Union created a totally different situation. But no one had a strategy or plan to exploit the new opportunities, and time was wasted. Good intentions but lack of strategy produced a backlash in Russia. The nation encountered serious problems, including difficult internal reforms. Meanwhile, the West concentrated on the immediate task of integrating the former Warsaw Pact members, which produced a negative response from Russia. It suspected it was being treated as a defeated nation, marginalized, and accorded second-rate status. Considerable efforts were needed to find a way out and to forestall abiding alienation between NATO and Russia.

It has also been true that relations between NATO and Russia—indeed, the security relationship as such between the West and Russia—represent only part of the interest that the West has in Russia's future and only part of the institutional responsibility for promoting Russia's integration in the outside world. As important as NATO-Russia relations are and will continue to be in the future, nonsecurity relations, especially economic relations, will acquire increasing importance. Indeed, the role of the European Union (EU) may become more important for Russia, and for Russian-Western relations, than anything that happens with NATO (or with the strictly "security" aspects of the EU, focusing on Common Foreign and Security Policy and the European Security and Defence Policy.) While these nonsecurity issues are beyond the scope of this study, they must still be borne in mind while reading the following analysis and recommendations. "Integration" of Russia into the outside world and, to some degree, in Western institutions is, in fact, all of a piece.

Just prior to NATO's decision in July 1997 to admit to membership the first three countries from the former Warsaw Pact (Poland, Hungary, and the Czech Republic), it concluded a Founding Act with the Russian Federation. In it, the two parties agreed

> [to] build together a lasting and inclusive peace in the Euro-Atlantic area on the principles of democracy and cooperative security.[1]

To that end, NATO and Russia created the Permanent Joint Council (PJC), which met at "19+1"—that is, with the North Atlantic Council assembled as a whole in meeting with a Russian representative. The PJC was designed

---

[1] Founding Act (1997).

to build increasing levels of trust, unity of purpose and habits of consultation and cooperation between NATO and Russia, in order to enhance each other's security and that of all nations in the Euro-Atlantic area and diminish the security of none. . . . [It] will provide a mechanism for consultations, coordination and, to the maximum extent possible, where appropriate, for joint decisions and joint action with respect to security issues of common concern.[2]

At the time, this was certainly an ambitious undertaking, less than a decade after the end of the Cold War. Indeed, when the Founding Act stated that "NATO and Russia do not consider each other as adversaries," this was for many observers a remarkable comment, not the commonplace it has now become. Further, the two parties agreed to embark on a wide range of cooperative activities in nineteen separate areas directly germane to security and confidence building, while also agreeing that "other areas can be added by mutual agreement."[3]

Despite the wide-ranging and comprehensive nature of the Founding Act, however, it was longer on rhetoric than on mutual hope that it could provide a firm basis for transforming the nature of the West's security relations with Russia. Both sides implicitly recognized that it was some form of political "compensation" to Russia—though never formally acknowledged as such—for the impending enlargement of NATO. Indeed, the early record of the PJC could be found more in meeting communiqués citing ambitions rather than solid achievements, which were as much outside the framework of the Founding Act—notably the engagement of Russian military forces as part of the NATO-led Implementation/ Stabilization Force in Bosnia, beginning even before the Founding Act in December 1995. And within two years of the Founding Act's adoption, NATO-Russia relations hit a major roadblock when the alliance began its 78-day air campaign against Serbia over Kosovo, to which Russia objected vigorously.

Nevertheless, the passage of time, the cooling of historical memories of Cold War confrontation, and Russia's gradual internal developments led the NATO-Russia relationship to begin acquiring something more than mere symbolic significance. As a reflection both of relations on the mend after Kosovo and of shared political, security, and strategic interests following the September 11, 2001, terrorist attacks in the United States, NATO and the Russian Federation, at a summit meeting in Rome in May 2002, agreed to take their relationship a step further:

opening a new page in our relations, aimed at enhancing our ability to work together in areas of common interest and to stand together against common threats and risks to our security.[4]

In practical terms, they agreed to create a NATO-Russia Council (NRC), "where NATO member states and Russia will work *as equal partners* in areas of common interest" [emphasis added].[5] Most important, the signatories agreed to drop the cumbersome proce-

---

[2] Founding Act (1997).

[3] See "Areas for Consultation and Cooperation," Section III in Founding Act (1997).

[4] Heads of State and Government of NATO Member States and the Russian Federation, "NATO-Russia Relations: A New Quality," declaration, Rome, Italy, May 2002; online at http://www.nato.int/docu/basictxt/b020528e.htm (as of September 22, 2004).

[5] "A New Quality" (2002). However, the goals of working together were virtually the same as for the PJC: "The NATO-Russia Council will provide a mechanism for consultation, consensus-building, cooperation, joint decision, and joint action

dures under which the PJC had been chaired—a "troika" consisting of the NATO Secretary General, the Russian Ambassador to Belgium (who represented Russia's interests at NATO), and an ambassador from a NATO nation, rotating monthly. The new NATO-Russia Council has only one chairman, the NATO Secretary-General—a sign of developing trust on the part of the Russians but also a signal that the NRC meets "at 20," not at "19+1," and, as with the North Atlantic Council, all decisions are taken by consensus. The symbolic, more than the substantive, quality of changing the PJC structure is important in terms of conveying the important matter of "equality" that has to define any NATO-Russian relationship that can hope to be effective and to endure.

Through these changes and their promise, engaging Russia within a NATO-based institution is no longer in any serious way "compensation" for NATO enlargement—actual or potential—but rather a development with merit and significance to all parties in its own right. At the same time, for NRC to succeed—indeed, for Russian-Western relations to succeed—most careful and conscientious efforts need to be made to keep NATO enlargement, present or future, from again becoming a matter of serious contention. In part, that argues for efforts, on the part of all concerned, at reconciliation (where it does not already exist) between the Russian Federation and the states that have joined NATO. This will impose responsibilities on all parties, and NATO, with its various institutions—including such forums as the Euro-Atlantic Partnership Council—can play an instrumental role in what is, at heart, essentially both a political and functional process.

This report does not review the record of the NATO-Russia Council since its inception in detail; that can be gleaned most effectively from NATO's formal presentations and the record that is continually being built upon.[6] This report highlights some signal achievements. Most notably, the council was not, unlike its PJC predecessor, effectively rendered obsolete politically by an external disruption to relations between Russia and (at least some of) the Western powers—in this case, the 2003 War in Iraq—as had happened during the 1999 Kosovo conflict. This report also points out some areas that the members of the RAND-ISKRAN NATO-Russia Working Group believe the NRC can usefully engage, beyond those already on the agenda to be pursued—itself an extensive agenda for cooperation.[7] Critical achievements, and the forward agenda, include the following[8]:

for the member states of NATO and Russia on a wide spectrum of security issues in the Euro-Atlantic region," and the eight areas singled out for cooperation had almost all been in the list of 19 areas of cooperation for the PJC: "[the] struggle against terrorism, crisis management, non-proliferation, arms control and confidence-building measures, theatre missile defence, search and rescue at sea, military-to-military cooperation, and civil emergencies." The two new additions were "struggle against terrorism" (understandably, with the sudden new interest after September 11) and "search and rescue at sea."

[6] See "A New Quality" (2002) and the supporting texts available on the following Web site: NATO Headquarters, NATO-Russia Relations: Building a Lasting and Inclusive Peace in the Euro-Atlantic Area, 8 September 2004; online at http://www.nato.int/issues/nato-russia/index.html (as of 22 September 2004). Most recently, in April 2004, Russia agreed to send military liaison officers to the two NATO headquarters, Allied Common Operations (SHAPE) in Mons, Belgium, and Allied Command Transformation in Norfolk, Virginia. See NATO Headquarters, "NATO and Russia Enhance Military Cooperation," NATO Update, April 16, 2004; online at http://www.nato.int/docu/update/2004/04-april/e0407c.htm (as of September 22, 2004). This step had been pending since the conclusion of the Founding Act in 1997.

[7] See, for instance, NATO Headquarters, Third NATO-Russia Conference on Terrorism, Web site, April 5, 2004; online at http://www.nato.int/docu/update/2004/04-april/e0405a.htm (as of 23 September 2004) and Chairman's Statement, Informal Meeting of the NATO-Russia Council at the Level of Foreign Ministers, April 2, 2004; online at http://www.nato.int/docu/pr/2004/p040402-nrc-e.htm (as of 23 September 2004).

[8] NATO-Russia Council, Meeting at the Level of Foreign Ministers, statement, Brussels: NATO Headquarters, 4 December 2003; online at http://www.nato.int/docu/pr/2003/p031204e.htm (as of September 23, 2004). Also see NATO-Russia

- further work on practical aspects of our fight against terrorism, building on agreed threat assessments;
- the broadening and deepening of NRC co-operation on defence reform;
- the intensification of NRC military-to-military co-operation and efforts to develop interoperability among NATO and Russian forces;
- progress made to date in implementation of the ongoing NATO-Russia Procedural Exercise, designed to address modalities for possible NATO-Russia Peacekeeping Operations, as well as other work aimed at improving our co-operation on peacekeeping;
- intensified co-operation in coping with civil emergencies, including Russia's invitation to NRC member states to participate in the exercise "Kaliningrad 2004";
- ongoing dialogue and co-operation on a range of nuclear issues, including Russia's invitation to NRC countries to observe a field exercise on safe handling procedures for nuclear weapons;
- the development of an experimental concept of TMD operations and the scheduling of a related Command Post Exercise in early 2004; and
- approval of the Co-operative Airspace Initiative Project Plan.

Collectively, these must be judged to be significant elements of a constructive, *functional* approach to building relations between Russia and the West, focused here on NATO as one institution (developing in parallel with Russia-EU relations and Russian relations with individual Western states). As was demonstrated even during the Cold War, working together on areas of mutual common interest (in those days centering on efforts to prevent the East-West political relationship from being determined by the state of the nuclear balance) can in time lead to significant changes in political relations, summarized as the product of "confidence-building measures." But by their very nature, these measures are bounded according to their own terms: On their own, they do not produce a redefinition of underlying strategic and political relations. That redefinition imposes its own requirements.

Whether the time has arrived for such a redefinition of Russia's relations with NATO—or *within* NATO, in the broadest sense of the Alliance and its ambitions—is the key point of today's discussions and of this report. This matter has two dimensions, which cannot be entirely separated from one another:

1. the fulfillment of a "20th century" security agenda, found in President George H.W. Bush's notion of a Europe "whole and free"—a notion that, more prosaically, can be summarized as the effort to create a basis for ensuring that the last century's European tragedy will "never again" be visited

2. a new agenda opening beyond Europe with the 21st century and typified by three concerns: terrorism, the spread of WMD, and security for—if not the transformation of—the "Broader Middle East," in the context of NATO-Russia relations a region roughly stretching from the Levant and the Persian Gulf to the Transcaucasus and Central Asia.

By the same token, the perspective now opening up in Russia's relations with the West, especially with NATO, has two distinct but overlapping elements:

Council, Meeting at the Level of Ministers of Defence, statement, Brussels: NATO Headquarters, December 1, 2003; online at http://www.nato.int/docu/pr/2003/p031201e.htm (as of September 23, 2004).

- Russia should participate more and in a more-integrated way in security, political, economic, and other arrangements for the great, ongoing experiment in determining security in "Europe" for the years ahead.
- Russia should take a role in the development of Western policy and practice in areas beyond Europe, including the definition of *security*. One definition, most clearly advanced by the United States, implies a deep and lasting engagement by Western countries and institutions in the Middle East (and potentially beyond), including the region's long-term transformation—both on the parts of individual states and collectively. Here, too, there will be both a need and an opportunity for Russian "consultations, coordination and, to the maximum extent possible, where appropriate, for joint decisions and joint action with respect to security issues of common concern."

The next phase of NATO's relations with Russia needs to focus on the latter's *engagement*. To complete the 20th-century agenda, that means deepening what Russia does with *NATO*, both politically and militarily—the original course of work for the PJC and the NRC. To open the 21st-century agenda, that means the development of NATO's involvement beyond Europe *at the same time and with a clear sense of cooperation and coordination* as the development of NATO-Russia relations. What the two do in Europe is, in essence, a way of adding Russia to a process that has long been under way, some elements since the end of the Cold War and some other basic elements since the origin of NATO. But what NATO does either on its own or together with Russia in what NATO used to call "out of area" has the potential of developing in a way that is reinforcing from the beginning and that can have the concept of "equality" built in. That does not mean that all interests and practices will be shared—far from it—but that there is a chance for NATO and Russia to work together on the ground, with the possibilities that that approach connotes.

What follows, therefore, analyzes and suggests means of Russian *engagement* with NATO, in the two great geographic realms of the Alliance's future activity and in various functional realms. How NATO and Russia perform in these realms will largely determine the nature of their future relations and the prospects for a cooperative future—indeed, for the fruition of a "Europe whole and free," in its broadest scope, insofar as that is determined by NATO and the Russian Federation.

CHAPTER TWO

NATO-Russia in Europe

Both the NATO-Russia Founding Act and the Rome declaration of heads of state and government in May 2002 on NATO-Russia relations were conceived more in terms of mutual challenges and cooperation in regard to Europe—"a wide spectrum of security issues in the Euro-Atlantic region" in the words of the latter agreement[1]—rather than territories (or threats) beyond the continent, or at least entailing actions beyond the continent. Even on terrorism, in agreeing to "strengthen cooperation through a multi-faceted approach, including joint assessments," this extended to "specific threats . . . to Russian and NATO forces" that were not otherwise delineated (e.g., threats taking place outside of Europe). Indeed, "an initial step will be a joint assessment of the terrorist threat to NATO, Russia and Partner peacekeeping forces *in the Balkans*" [emphasis added].[2]

Thus, the first task of the "new NATO-Russian relationship" has naturally focused on what is possible and desirable within the traditional compass of NATO and of Russia's emerging relations with NATO: in effect, the area in Europe delimited by Article 6 of the North Atlantic Treaty,[3] plus the newer areas of operation in the first definition for NATO of "outside of area" (i.e., the Balkans) and even beyond, including the global perspective of the Proliferation Working Group.

Following the Rome declaration and the creation of the NATO-Russia Council, the NATO-Russia Working Group judged that a few key areas need to be emphasized in terms of the "European" dimension of work to be done. In some of these areas, efforts are already in train; in others, not yet. We discuss them in the following sections according to general function.

Personnel Engagement, Exchanges, and Staffing

Historically, one of NATO's great strengths has been the fact that a large number of diplomatic and military personnel of the various allied states have worked together on common functions, beginning with NATO Headquarters and fanning out through the military com-

---

[1] A New Quality (2002)

[2] From A New Quality (2002):

> Struggle Against Terrorism: strengthen cooperation through a multi-faceted approach, including joint assessments of the terrorist threat to the Euro-Atlantic area, focused on specific threats, for example, to Russian and NATO forces, to civilian aircraft, or to critical infrastructure; an initial step will be a joint assessment of the terrorist threat to NATO, Russia and Partner peacekeeping forces in the Balkans.

[3] See The North Atlantic Treaty, Washington D.C., April 4, 1949; online at http://www.nato.int/docu/basictxt/treaty.htm (as of 23 September 2004).

mands and ancillary activities (e.g., in planning, logistics, command and control, even basic science). The degree to which this interaction, including the "magic" of Allied Commands Europe and Atlantic,[4] has determined the politics of the Alliance cannot be judged but is surely considerable. Along with such factors as the North Atlantic Council's consensus rule—now adopted as well for NATO-Russia decisionmaking—this constant, daily interaction has helped contribute to a signal fact: NATO has never failed to carry through a decision. Indeed, during both the Bosnia and Kosovo conflicts, there were deep divisions within the Alliance. Yet, once the allies reached consensus on these conflicts, none departed from it.

An important element of developing NATO-Russia relations (as in developing NATO relations with other members of the Euro-Atlantic Partnership Council [EAPC] and Partnership for Peace [PFP]) thus lies in the functional engagement of Russian and NATO officials, personnel (civilian and military), and staffs with one another. Of course, this is not the be-all and end-all. But this continual, quotidian interaction can be of high value, both now and in the future. This was certainly proved by the direct engagement of Russian forces in NATO-led peacekeeping operations in Bosnia (IFOR and SFOR) and Kosovo (KFOR). In this context, one of the most significant innovations of the NATO-Russia Council has been the creation of a preparatory committee, at the level of political counselors, which provides a forum for regular, relatively informal exchanges of views on political issues and avenues of practical cooperation. The fact that a total of 17 subordinate committees, working groups, and expert groups (as compared with two for the PJC), each creating a distinct community of stakeholders in NATO-Russia cooperation, support the NRC is also a step forward.

Some key areas for development (partly achieved, partly in train, partly further initiatives) are as follows:

- Top-level Russian diplomatic personnel should increasingly be engaged in Brussels and at the key NATO commands, the latter personnel to act in liaison with the political advisors to the NATO commanders. There should likewise be reciprocal engagement of top-level allied (NATO) diplomatic personnel with appropriate institutions in Russia, not just with the formal NATO office in Moscow but also at the Foreign Ministry and other establishments, as appropriate.
- Similarly, as has been developing recently, direct engagement of both senior-level and "tactical"-level Russian and allied military personnel in one another's respective command headquarters (as well as at NATO-Brussels and in the Russian defense ministry) should increase. This engagement—including personnel "exchanges" for purposes of joint staff training and development of common or compatible doctrines (e.g., for peacemaking and peacekeeping)—should also extend to newer command structures that both Russian military and NATO develop, and especially the new NATO Response Force (NRF). The last step should take place rapidly, even before decisions are made about whether Russia—and potentially other non-NATO-member states in the EAPC/PFP—will be invited to participate formally in the NRF, including its planning, training, and command functions; force generation; and deployment and employment.

---

[4] Now replaced by Allied Commands Operations and Transformation.

- Increasingly, NATO has been involving Russian civilian and military personnel in its regular staff and committee structure. While, there are areas in which it may not be appropriate to engage Russian personnel (e.g., in many NATO intelligence exchanges), at least while mutual confidence (and mutual interests) are developing, the goal should be for *inclusion* to become the rule and *exclusion* the exception. (At the same time, of course, a similar practice needs to be extended, as appropriate, to other members of EAPC/PFP, in part so that confidence-building for one does not reduce the confidence of another.)
- In parallel, with EU agreement, Russian civilian and military observers should be included in NATO's formal work with the EU, including relations with the Common Foreign and Security Policy (CFSP) and—especially—the European Security and Defence Policy (ESDP). Given that the relationship between NATO and ESDP includes assumptions that the latter's activities must be viewed in the light of possible escalation or hand-off to the former, it would be appropriate for Russia to have at least a watching brief. In developing its own relations with Russia, the EU should keep Moscow informed of progress on CFSP and ESDP, some of which could done trilaterally.

In pursuing each of these areas of cooperation, it is especially important that NATO, in its deliberations, increasingly seek counsel from Russian representatives early in any crisis—and that, for its part, Russia do likewise regarding any foreign policy crisis it may face. As with other members of the EAPC/PFP, such engagement must no longer be seen as an afterthought but as an integral and necessary part both of NATO's day-to-day success and of the longer-term achievement of the underlying goal of creating a "Europe whole and free."

Military-to-Military Cooperation

More than any other factor, NATO-Russia cooperation is about political engagement. This will largely define what is possible, in terms of progressively developing common (or at least fully compatible) views about European security and creating a solid basis for ensuring the emergence of a "Europe whole and free." But these statements also relate to other aspects of Russian engagement with the West, including with the EU. NATO's signal contributions are that, more than any other Western institution, it is the primary institutional link between Europe and North America; it is the repository of strategic purpose for Europe; and its expression of these purposes includes the maintenance of robust military forces, Allied Commands Operations and Transformation, and the "all for one and one for all" mutual defense commitments of the NATO Treaty's Article 5.[5] Yet, like other members of the EAPC/PFP, Russia is excluded from these aspects of NATO's role as a nonsignatory of the treaty.

---

[5] From the North Atlantic Treaty (1949):

> The Parties agree that an armed attack against one or more of them in Europe or North America shall be considered an attack against them all and consequently they agree that, if such an armed attack occurs, each of them, in exercise of the right of individual or collective self-defence recognised by Article 51 of the Charter of the United Nations [UN], will assist the Party or Parties so attacked by taking forthwith, individually and in concert with the other Parties, such action as it deems necessary, including the use of armed force, to restore and maintain the security of the North Atlantic area. . . .

Thus, a good deal of the development of Russia's *political* and *strategic* relations with the West, beyond its bilateral relations with key countries in Europe and North America, depends on what happens in terms of its military relationship with NATO, its institutions and practices, and its actions. This military relationship cannot be permitted to lag behind the political steps; indeed, there have already been some of what might be considered setbacks, including the withdrawal of Russian forces from IFOR (June 2003)[6] and KFOR (July 2003).[7] However, these forces, during the 7 and 4 years, respectively, that they took part in NATO-led peacekeeping, had an exemplary record.

It is impossible to define how much is enough at any point in NATO-Russia military-to-military relations and cooperation. Most important is that the pace be consistent with political intentions and ability to follow through—recognizing that the more Russians and NATO cadres have experience in working together, the more likely (other factors being equal) that the overall political relationship will prosper. Some key areas for development (partly achieved, partly in train, partly further initiatives) are as follows:

- Russian staff planners and military experts should be progressively consulted and engaged in developing NATO peacekeeping doctrine, including the employment doctrine for NRF—recognizing, of course, the requirements for engaging other EAPC/PFP countries. A viable vehicle for such an effort already exists, in the form of the Generic Concept for NATO-Russia Peacekeeping Operations," whose political decisionmaking aspects were agreed on in October 2002. This should develop into a corpus of common doctrine, developed as a two-way street and to be drawn upon by a wide range of "NATO-family" countries.

- Russia should create significant officer and enlisted training opportunities for NATO personnel in Russia, to parallel Russian participation in NATO and NATO-related schools, such as the Marshall Center, the NATO School at Oberammergau, and the NATO Defence College in Rome. There should also be increased opportunities for Russian officers to attend allied defense schools; increased exchanges of experience in solving practical military technical, planning, training, and logistical problems; and enhanced efforts to take advantage of the expertise gained by alumni of such exchanges. Some initial efforts have been made within the framework of NRC Working Groups on Peacekeeping and Defence Reform, but such programs should be expanded.

- Now that Russia has increased its participation in practical PFP activities, it should have a greater role—consonant with the interests of other members—in the work of the Partnership Coordination Cell. In general, NATO exercises, including command-post exercises, should increasingly focus on engagement of EAPC/PFP countries, with a heavy emphasis on what Russia, as far and away the leading non-NATO EAPC military power, has to contribute, including to the definition and planning of exercises. It was notable, for example, that the latest major NATO headquarters crisis exercise, CMX-04 in March 2004, dealt with Russia (or other EAPC states) only in a cursory way—indeed, as an afterthought, even though characteristics of the exercise

---

[6] Viktor Nikolla, "The Last Farewell from the Russians," 20 June 2003; online at http://www.nato.int/sfor/indexinf/articles/030620c/t030620c.htm (as of September 23, 2004).

[7] NATO Headquarters, "Russian Troops Leave KFOR," NATO Update, July 2, 2003; online at http://www.nato.int/docu/update/2003/07-july/e0702a.htm (as of 23 September 2004).

"notionally" engaged Russian interests. Lack of attention to Russia's interests and concerns, symbolized by this event, makes many Russian observers deeply suspicious of NATO's attitude.

- The logical—and political—implication of increased military-to-military cooperation and experience, as well as of an evolving political relationship, is that Russia should increasingly be considered—and Russia should consider itself—part of NATO deployment and employment. Obviously, this concept will depend on the degree to which Western and Russian strategic and political interests are compatible and reinforcing, which will not always be the case (see Chapter Three), a judgment that often cannot be made in advance. Within these limitations, however, Russia should increasingly participate (with other EAPC states) in the practical workings of NATO-run Combined Joint Task Force (CJTF) headquarters and in NRF. Given that the latter will depend heavily on force-generation processes and is already being configured to be as much "plug and play" as possible—i.e., to enable individual allied countries to opt out of particular operations without jeopardizing the ability to carry out those operations—Russia can be a participant, and both NATO and Russia should work toward that end. Indeed, after an initial cycle of NRF training that passes through lead nations in the Alliance, NATO and Russia should consider giving Russia a lead-nation role in one of the rotations.

Transformation, Interoperability, and Defense Industrial Relations

Military equipment and other materiel are not just the sinews of war but a key factor in determining whether and how the militaries of different countries can work together. At NATO, Allied Command Europe (now Operations) has been the key mechanism for drawing the different allied militaries together and keeping them together. At the same time, NATO has always focused on developing common procedures and command-and-control arrangements (today encompassing all elements of C^4ISR—command, control, communications, computers, intelligence, surveillance, and reconnaissance). In these areas, the Alliance has been highly successful; progressively acquainting Russian forces with these *processes* is part not just of their being able to work effectively *with* and *within* NATO but also of developing habits of mind and behavior that can have positive political effects.

At the same time, NATO has long focused on the importance of making its forces, equipment, and techniques *interoperable*. Ideally, that word implies interchangeability, as in ammunition and fuels. Less ideally, it implies at least compatibility— that the different militaries can fight together. At this, NATO has always been less successful, in part because of the desires of different allies to manufacture equipment for their national use (if not also allied use) in their own national factories. While not desirable militarily, it has been part of sustaining national support for defense efforts and participation within an alliance, rather than going one's own way.

In today's and tomorrow's military environment, accepting compatibility as the standard for interoperability is no longer good enough. The emphasis now has to be on integration (or integratability), for several reasons, of which three stand out:

1. Emphasis on expeditionary forces (as in IFOR/SFOR, KFOR, ISAF, and generically through the NRF) has been increasing within NATO. At no time during the Cold War

was there a need to put together forces that would actually fight together, as opposed to train together and take part in exercises together.

2. Emphasis on small-unit interaction between the forces of different allied nations, as opposed to the division- or even corps-level relationship during the Cold War, has also been increasing. This puts an added premium on the capacity of forces to work directly together at the lowest tactical levels.

3. Allied forces are transforming themselves at significantly different rates, with the United States clearly in the lead. This has actually exacerbated the problem of interoperability and in some cases increased the difficulties of common allied military action—as witnessed, for example, in Kosovo. One partial answer is to focus on C^4ISR. But this will increasingly be inadequate for the modern battlefield.

All these factors will clearly have a major influence on the ability of Russian forces to be able to work effectively with NATO forces and, in addition, on the development of Russian strategic, political, and industrial relations with NATO and NATO countries. This will be important in many ways, several of which particularly so. Some key areas for development (partly achieved, partly in train, partly further initiatives) are as follows:

- For more than a decade, the Russian Federation has expressed concern that NATO enlargement would impose an added penalty of losing a traditional market, as former Warsaw Pact countries shift from Soviet-made and -standard weapons to those of the NATO alliance. This has indeed happened to some extent, as would have happened even without either NATO enlargement or the PFP. However, Russia—along with Ukraine—does retain some markets for repairing Warsaw Pact equipment (e.g., MiG-29 aircraft) that has not yet been replaced. In fact, Russia has found some markets (including for transport aircraft and technological upgrades) that might not have existed if NATO were not pressuring candidate states to modernize their forces in the context of the Membership Action Plan (MAP) process. Russia is also trying to sell military hardware to China, India, and other non-Western countries. Beyond the very short term, however, Russia has little choice but to begin adopting NATO standards if it hopes to produce equipment that can be attractive to other European states. NATO has opened up some NATO standardization agreements (STANAGS) to Russia, which has adopted some of them. More will be needed. As this happens, the West will need to address the problem of releasing higher technology data to Russia, which will, in turn, have to demonstrate that it can be trusted not to pass the data on to third parties.

- These issues can addressed in part by fully implementing the provision in the NATO-Russia Founding Act that provides for "pursuing possible armaments-related cooperation through association of Russia with NATO's Conference of National Armaments Directors" (CNAD), where there has so far been limited engagement.[8] In parallel, the EU should explore a relationship with Russia in the context of the West

---

[8] Founding Act (2002). For a description of the CNAD, see NATO Headquarters, "Key to Organisations and Agencies and Other Subordinate Bodies—Production Logistics and Equipment: Conference of National Armaments Directors (CNAD)," *NATO Handbook*, 4 November 2002, Chapter 14; online at http://www.nato.int/docu/handbook/2001/hb140301.htm (as of September 23, 2004). Among steps taken, Russia has participated in talks about submarine accidents. See NATO Headquarters, "Armaments Directors Hold Biannual Meeting," NATO Update, 13 November 2003; online at http://www.nato.int/docu/update/2003/11-november/e1105b.htm (as of September 23, 2004).

European Armaments Group/Organisation (WEAG/WEAO) and other appropriate bodies. These steps would promote the necessary dialogue on the ways in which Russia can both develop its own defense industries in ways that will support compatibility with NATO military equipment and better understand what it needs to do to have access to NATO markets. Further, NATO and Russia should associate the latter with the Defence Capabilities Commitment adopted at the Prague Summit in October 2002,[9] making Russia eligible to compete in providing as wide a range of equipment as possible. Russia could also be associated with the EU's European Capabilities Action Plan (ECAP).

- At the same time, Russia should be progressively associated, both politically and militarily, with NATO transformation, including cutting-edge work being done at Allied Command Transformation, consistent with security requirements. The goal should be for *inclusion* to become the expectation and *exclusion* the exception. For example, NATO should consider according Russia a role in the development of its Allied Ground Surveillance project on a "user" basis and, in a later iteration, actually providing some of the equipment. At the same time, Russia should share its transformation work with NATO and engage NATO with its development. The concept of working toward *inclusion* not *exclusion* on both sides would help to promote NATO-Russia military cooperation that has a sound basis in practical engagement, in which Russian military forces would be better able to integrate with NATO's in the kind of operations that are most likely to define NATO's future.
- In terms of practical experience in implementing these measures, Russia will need to become more responsive to NATO requests for participation in military exercises and—consistent with Moscow's political decisions—deployments (e.g., as in Bosnia and Kosovo), as well for NATO to make such opportunities possible.

Civil Emergencies

For nearly a decade, NATO has cooperated with the Russian Federation in one particular area of special significance: civil emergency preparedness. For its part, the Alliance has long had its Senior Civil Emergency Planning Committee (SCEPC), which is also part of the broader European Euro-Atlantic Disaster Relief Coordinating Committee (EADRCC). And Russia, for its part, has had its Ministry of Emergency Situations, which has had the same minister for the past 13 years, General of the Army Sergey Shoygu. This cooperation in civil emergency preparedness has been particularly successful in part because it has so few political

---

[9] For a description of the initiative, see Heads of State and Government Participating in the Meeting of the North Atlantic Council, Prague Summit Declaration, Prague, November 21, 2002; online at http://www.nato.int/docu/pr/2002/p02-127e.htm (as of 23 September 2004):

> 4 . . . We have therefore decided to: . . . c. Approve the Prague Capabilities Commitment (PCC) as part of the continuing Alliance effort to improve and develop new military capabilities for modern warfare in a high threat environment. Individual Allies have made firm and specific political commitments to improve their capabilities in the areas of chemical, biological, radiological, and nuclear defence; intelligence, surveillance, and target acquisition; air-to-ground surveillance; command, control and communications; combat effectiveness, including precision guided munitions and suppression of enemy air defences; strategic air and sea lift; air-to-air refuelling; and deployable combat support and combat service support units. Our efforts to improve capabilities through the PCC and those of the European Union to enhance European capabilities through the European Capabilities Action Plan should be mutually reinforcing, while respecting the autonomy of both organisations, and in a spirit of openness.

aspects; in this area, working together does not pose or beg any larger questions. At the same time, for both NATO countries and for Russia, it is an area of governmental action that lies close to the interests and needs of individual people and communities. Indeed, in the area of natural disasters—fire, flood, earthquake—governments have unavoidable responsibilities and are held accountable by the citizens of a nation. This responsibility is independent of ideology, ethnicity, and religion.

SCEPC was initially designed largely to coordinate NATO-nation efforts within allied territory in the event of a war; it was only secondarily about natural disasters. Today, the first requirement has essentially disappeared. At the same time, concern is rising about the possibilities of terrorism or other civil destruction (in addition to natural disasters), a concern all members of the NATO-Russia Council increasingly share.[10]

Civil emergency preparedness is thus an area in which NATO-Russia cooperation can readily be extended, with a direct effects both on the lives of peoples and communities and, one can expect, on attitudes on both sides toward further extending this cooperation. A combined civil emergency-preparedness organization could act in several areas:

- common staffing of headquarters and planning work
- development of joint doctrine
- combining of relevant capabilities
- sharing of intelligence
- exercises
- joint deployments to natural disasters (and potentially to terrorist sites).

As noted, the success of this venture could have positive benefits on public opinion in NATO countries and in Russia about the overall relationship. It could also provide lessons in practical areas of cooperation, including the paramilitary area, that could be applied elsewhere. In particular, this cooperation could become a basis for developing joint capacities for "nation-building," as applied to post-crisis requirements, as in Afghanistan and Iraq.

Arms Control: The Treaty on Conventional Armed Forces in Europe

Ongoing disagreements over issues related to the Treaty on Conventional Armed Forces in Europe (CFE) continue to cast a cloud over the NATO-Russia relationship out of all proportion to the technical nature of the questions themselves and despite the relatively modest steps each side would need to take to address the other's concerns.

NATO continues to insist on full implementation of the political commitments (which are not legally binding) that Russia undertook at the 1999 Istanbul OSCE Summit to resolve questions related to compliance with treaty host-state consent requirements in Georgia and Moldova. The following are among the remaining unfulfilled "Istanbul commitments":

---

[10] In March 2004, for the first time, the annual NATO headquarters crisis management exercise—CMS-04—was based on a scenario that centered on a terrorist incident: a hypothetical explosion at a chemical plant in the Netherlands. While the notional crisis did not affect Russia directly, it established the principle that Russia could be affected by such an event, as well as Russia's potential interest in the notional source of the terrorism, a nonexistent country close to Russian territory.

- in Moldova: the withdrawal and destruction of roughly 37 trainloads of munitions at a Russian base in Colbasna (Transdniestria) and the withdrawal of approximately 950 Russian personnel charged with guarding these munitions and overseeing the process of withdrawal and destruction[11]
- in Georgia: the conclusion of a Russo-Georgian basing agreement that defines the terms and duration of the Russian military presence in Georgia.

For its part, Russia insists on the immediate ratification of the Agreement on Adaptation of the CFE Treaty (also concluded by the treaty's 30 party states at the 1999 Istanbul Summit), to allow the accession of the four new NATO member states (Estonia, Latvia, Lithuania, and Slovenia), which are not currently parties to the treaty.[12] At the same time, Russia wants to resolve the problems through bilateral arrangements with Moldova and Georgia. Russia claims that, besides some economic problems, an immediate withdrawal of its forces could result in serious destabilization of these countries, which suffered greatly in the 1990s during bloody ethnic-civil wars. All NATO governments, however, in signing the adaptation agreement, made clear that they would submit it to their respective national parliaments for ratification only after the Russian commitments (designed to bring Russia into compliance with the core host-state consent provisions of the treaty's Article IV) were implemented. The NATO position aside, the entry into force of the adapted treaty would require its ratification by all 30 CFE states, including Georgia and Moldova, whose assent is unlikely absent resolution of the "Istanbul" issues.

The remaining steps that both sides need to take are relatively modest and technical. Russia needs to relocate relatively small numbers of troops and amounts of equipment from Moldova and needs to agree on the time frame and modalities for the withdrawal of Russian forces and equipment from Georgia.[13] For NATO, the accession of the four non-CFE allies to the Treaty would largely codify existing political assurances of restraint that exist in the NATO-Russia Founding Act and elsewhere. Yet the persistence of this dispute continues to play into the hands of those on both sides most critical of NATO-Russia cooperation: For Russian populist politicians, the inapplicability of legally binding CFE limitations in the Baltic region fuels the notion of "encirclement"—a hostile NATO that can move unlimited numbers of troops and equipment to Russia's borders (whether that intention exists or not). By the same token, however, some of the new NATO allies see the prolonged delay in implementation of the Russian Istanbul commitments—which, after all, involve the presence of Russian forces on the territory of states that do not necessarily want them there—through the prism of their own experiences with Soviet forces on their territory. This too feeds suspicion of Russia's motives and serves to obstruct NATO-Russia cooperation.

---

[11] An additional 350 Russian personnel are present in Moldova under the terms of a 1992 cease-fire agreement between Chisinau and Tiraspol. How many, if any, of these forces would remain is linked to ongoing negotiations over a political settlement to the Transdniestria conflict, and it is a matter for interpretation whether they are included in the Istanbul commitment to complete withdrawal.

[12] The original 1990 Treaty was conceived as a bloc-to-bloc arrangement designed to ensure parity between the forces of NATO and those of the Warsaw Pact—it therefore did not contain an accession clause, one of many changes agreed on in 1999 to update the treaty to the new Euro-Atlantic security environment. The three Baltic states never became parties to the treaty, since they have never considered themselves to be "successor states" to the Soviet Union. Slovenia, as a former Yugoslav republic, was never part of the Warsaw Pact and therefore not included in the original treaty.

[13] The prospect seems much more likely after the November 2003 change of government in Tbilisi and Russian cooperation in returning Ajaria to Georgian control.

Both sides need to take concrete and expeditious steps toward ending this long-standing dispute. Despite philosophical disputes over whether the Istanbul commitments are formally "linked" to the CFE Treaty, Western members of Working Group believe that only Russian implementation of remaining commitments would clear the way for the adapted treaty's ratification and entry into force, while Russian members do not share that opinion.

At the same time, continued uncertainty over the entry into force of the adapted treaty risks undermining the integrity of the CFE regime itself, which all members of the NRC agree is a valuable cornerstone of European security. Both sides need to move beyond finger pointing. They should concentrate on practical ways in which NATO member states and the Alliance itself might facilitate implementation, including expansion of financial assistance for the withdrawal process. Ensuring the sovereignty and independence of newly independent states of the former Soviet Union, such as Moldova and Georgia, could require additional efforts, possibly including—in the case of Moldova—an NRC peacekeeping mission to monitor an eventual constitutional settlement.

The problems with the CFE Treaty demonstrate that arms control cannot be the main basis for Russia-NATO relationship. Only much greater political and military cooperation and joint activities can create a lasting and enduring security partnership. That does not mean that the CFE Treaty should be forgotten simply because Russia and the West are no longer enemies. It is still useful to create greater transparency and confidence. But arms control is not the end point in Russia-NATO relationship because, in the 21st century, the main task is to develop rules for cooperation, as opposed to Cold War–type efforts to regulate competition.

CHAPTER THREE
NATO-Russia Beyond Europe

The Political and Geopolitical Context

When the NATO-Russia Founding Act was signed, the compass of NATO activity was still very much bounded by geographic Europe. Except for the new relationship with Russia and some programs in EAPC and PFP, the limits of this geography only went as far as Central Europe. "Out of area" for NATO then meant Bosnia; it was still nearly two years before the term came to embrace Kosovo, as a sphere of action, then Macedonia; it was still longer before the "European" barrier was itself broken. NATO activity—and, hence, that to be contemplated in the new NATO-Russia relationship—was also bound functionally. Preventing the proliferation of WMD had been on the NATO agenda since 1991 (actively, since the Brussels Summit of January 1994) but had still not taken center stage or been a dynamic concern. And although the list of challenges in the Founding Act that PJC needed to face included both WMD proliferation and terrorism, neither was prominent. Also, for NATO as a whole and as late as the new NATO Strategic Concept adopted at the Washington Summit in May 1999, terrorism was only barely mentioned, meriting only four words: "Alliance security interests can be affected by other risks of a wider nature, *including acts of terrorism . . .*" [emphasis added].[1]

For NATO—and, by implication, for NATO-Russia—so much changed on September 11, 2001, and even more with the 2003 War in Iraq.[2] Russia insisted that terrorism had been the top-priority threat even before then. The creation of the NATO-Russia Council and the broadening of its agenda have already been discussed. But it is not just that both WMD and terrorism, as matters of common interest, are now on NATO's and NATO-Russia's agendas (to different degrees), it is also that the locus of common concern has extended radically beyond the classic areas of critical Russian-Western interaction in Europe.[3] Regarding terrorism, Russia extended significant cooperation to the United States and (by incorporation) to the West as a whole, including facilitating U.S. military deploy-

[1] From NATO, "The Alliance's Strategic Concept," Washington D.C., press release, NAC-S(99)65, April 24, 1999; online at http://www.nato.int/docu/pr/1999/p99-065e.htm (as of 23 September 2004):

24 . . . Alliance security must also take account of the global context. Alliance security interests can be affected by other risks of a wider nature, including acts of terrorism, sabotage and organised crime, and by the disruption of the flow of vital resources. The uncontrolled movement of large numbers of people, particularly as a consequence of armed conflicts, can also pose problems for security and stability affecting the Alliance.

[2] Notably, Russian President Vladimir Putin was the first foreign leader to telephone U.S. President George Bush on September 11, 2001.

[3] Of course, there had long been interaction in areas marked by the Great Game, as well as generally second-level confrontation between the Soviet Union and the West in areas now very much in play, including Turkey, Afghanistan, Iran, and other parts of the Middle East.

ments in Central Asian countries and intelligence sharing, including about Afghanistan. In exchange, the United States was more willing to accept fundamental aspects of Russian policy in Chechnya and to support efforts to counter terrorism in Georgia's Pankisi Gorge.

The key issues of WMD and terrorism have brought forth a natural agenda for bilateral U.S.-Russian relations and, as NATO extends its own geographic reach, for NATO-Russia relations—an agenda created by circumstance and necessity rather than a desire to work together. Russia and both the United States and NATO as a whole need to create a large body of workable political and practical stretching over a great swath of territory, from the edge of lands covered by the NATO treaty's Article 6 to the Afghan-Chinese border.

Russia is and will be a key player in Asia, where the main security challenges exist today. Without Russia, it would be difficult to deal with numerous hotbeds of tension from the Near East to the Korean Peninsula. This point has to be recognized but should not be misinterpreted.

At the very least, there has to be agreement that there will be no attempt in the 21st century to define areas of relative "dominant interest," as was common particularly in the 19th century, or to create a new "Great Game," in which regional countries are subjects of great-power politics. The West and Russia are rapidly closing the book on this kind of politics in Central Europe, and neither should have an interest in renewing it in Asia.

But having said what the rules should *not* be, it is even more important to determine what they *should* be. This will not be easy or automatic. In many areas—e.g., Central Asia and the Transcaucasus—Western (including NATO) experience is very recent, dating only from the 1991 creation of the North Atlantic Cooperation Council (NACC). There is significant possibility for mistakes and misunderstanding. The differences of view on Chechnya are a case in point, as are Russia's continuing military role in Georgia and the intentions of NATO and the United States in Central Asia.

At the same time, in the aftermath of the wars in Afghanistan and Iraq, it is clear that the United States and other Western powers will be involved in these countries (and other parts of the greater Middle East) for many years if not decades—certainly politically if not also militarily. Under a UN mandate, which Russia supported, NATO has already assumed responsibility for the International Security Assistance Force (ISAF) in Afghanistan and is increasing its responsibilities. NATO has also been playing a role in supporting individual allied force contributions in Iraq and is likely to assume some significant direct role in the future. Furthermore, NATO could also play a monitoring, peacekeeping, or other peace-enhancing role following a peace agreement between Israel and Palestine.

But what of Russia in all this? This question has three principal parts:

1. To what extent does NATO's engagement (and the fact of major change in the region itself) directly affect Russia's interests, which the West must take into account?

2. What are the shared interests and possibilities for direct cooperation in the security and other problems and challenges of countries in the region and of the region as a whole? (With regard to the Arab-Israeli conflict, this includes diplomatic issues.)

3. What are the implications of such NATO-Russian cooperation and of NATO's foray into this region as a whole, for the evolution of the Russia-NATO relationship across the board, including such issues as military-to-military relations, military doctrine, training, equipment, interoperability, and deployment, as well as the process of making decisions about the use of force?

All these are central questions for the future of NATO-Russia relations that must be answered as a matter both of necessity (to avoid problems in these relations) and of opportunity.

Ironically, NATO is today protecting Russia's "soft southern underbelly" in Afghanistan. But many observers, both in Russia and in the West, still do not admit this. The Working Group believes it is time to admit the new reality, which is totally different from the Cold War, openly.

The Working Group draws two important conclusions:

1. NATO's engagement in Asian territories bordering on Russia is not detrimental to Russia's security interests, and there is an urgent need for NATO-Russian cooperation and even potential joint action in and around these territories.
2. Dealing with the full range of concerns and possibilities about Afghanistan, Iraq, and other parts of the Middle East (including the zone of Arab-Israeli conflict) should involve political-level discussion and agreement (especially in the NATO-Russia Council) and practical steps in on-the-ground political, security, and military cooperation.

What follows is a discussion of these approaches in five critical areas in the region.

A Russian Role with NATO on Afghanistan

NATO's leadership of the UN-mandated International Security Assistance Force (ISAF) mission in Afghanistan is an opportunity for NATO-Russian cooperation. NATO and Russia have mutual interests in ensuring the stability of Afghanistan and in curbing the activities of terrorist and international drug-trafficking organizations. The NATO-Russia Council has already recognized the value of this cooperation. For example, the NATO Research and Technology Agency and the Russian State Committee for Control over the Illegal Trafficking of Narcotics and Psychotropic Substances are jointly examining the consequences of drug trafficking out of Afghanistan. But there is also scope for much broader cooperation, since the volume of drug traffic has unfortunately increased greatly since the destruction of the Taliban regime. This development has been of great concern to Russia and its Central Asian and European neighbors. And the terrorist threat continues.

NATO and Russia, whose forces are deployed near Afghanistan, should consider Russian participation in ISAF, in some form, to assist the Afghan Transitional Authority in maintaining security and to help ensure a safe environment within ISAF's area of responsibility. Russian forces and other military components should perhaps not be deployed for any length of time in Afghanistan, but they could undertake a wide range of operational missions, primarily from outside of Afghanistan, such as the following:

- helping monitor Afghanistan's borders
- combating drug trafficking and terrorism
- helping refugees return to Afghanistan
- contributing to intelligence collection, assessment, and coordination
- improving the capabilities of Afghanistan's police and armed forces by providing training and equipment
- assisting in general reconstruction efforts.

To engage with the NATO-led ISAF in these ways, the Russian civilian and military delegations at NATO Headquarters, along with their SHAPE counterparts, would have to develop a special command-and-control arrangement for Russian forces (perhaps using the Deputy to SACEUR for Russian Forces, whom Russia should appoint), agree to a set of guiding principles for NATO and Russian peacekeeping operations, identify the specific Russian area of responsibility, and outline the fundamental military tasks for Russian participation in antidrug and antiterrorist operations. Furthermore, it will be necessary to develop a process for Russia to participate in ISAF-related decisionmaking that would affect the roles and responsibilities of—and risks to—Russian forces. Carefully delimited and agreed on areas of activities could be worked out through the NATO-Russia Council. Indeed, this could become a means of testing and validating the worth of the NRC, in practical circumstances, as both allies and Russians consider the degree to which they are prepared to make concrete the agreed aspirations of making decisions and acting jointly on security issues of common concern.

Finding a practical way to incorporate Russia into ISAF, in ways that meet the needs of both NATO and Russia, would have several benefits.[4] First, NATO and Russia share a mutual interest in ensuring the stability of Afghanistan and in combating terrorist and drug-trafficking organizations operating in the country. Over 90 percent of heroin that Russian customs and border guards seize has been smuggled into Russia from Afghanistan through Tajikistan, Uzbekistan, Kyrgyzstan, Turkmenistan, and Kazakhstan. But these seizures are only a fraction of the heroin that gets through. Second, Russia's geographic proximity to and history of involvement in Afghanistan provide strong incentives for NATO to involve Russia in reconstruction efforts, rather than to work at odds with it. Russia is a major power in the region. It provides economic and very important military assistance to the Northern Front, and it took part in the December 2001 Bonn negotiations to create an interim political authority and set up a *loya jirga*. Since the Afghan government remains weak and the country is divided, Russia will continue to play a significant role in Afghanistan's future. It would be much more beneficial for NATO and Russia to cooperate than to compete.

There may, however, be obstacles to the integration of Russian military and other personnel into ISAF. Perhaps the most significant is the potential reaction in Afghanistan. Furthermore, Russians are not enthusiastic about sending soldiers to that country again. Will there be strong resistance to Russian participation because of the Soviet Union's invasion and subsequent war in Afghanistan? The answer may depend on whether NATO and Russia can reassure the Afghan government and population that Russian participation does not pose a threat to them. Other potential obstacles include language barriers (especially Russian command of English), a status of forces agreement (Russia concluded an unprecedented transit agreement with Germany but not with NATO), and interoperability of equipment and systems.

---

[4] On a bilateral basis, the United States and Russia could consider a role for the latter's Special Forces in Afghanistan, alongside the United States, French, British, and Australians.

A Russian Role in Iraq

Unlike the war in Kosovo, Russia was not alone in opposing the war in Iraq. Some "old" NATO members were even more critical. To some extent, that was a serious challenge to the cohesion of the Western alliance. But more recent developments, including the new UN Security Council resolution, created a new situation. What is required today is much stronger cooperation in Iraq, which, among other things, would strengthen the post–September 11 antiterrorist coalition.

The period following the transition from the U.S.-led Coalition Provisional Authority to a sovereign Iraqi government has been presenting a potential opportunity for NATO-Russian cooperation, even if, militarily, this is primarily for training Iraqi security forces.

Many NATO countries have already been playing important roles in helping to stabilize and rebuild Iraq. Integrating Russia into the postconflict reconstruction phase as NATO (and other Western) efforts potentially expand could be beneficial for both sides. First, because of Russia's interests in this region near its southern frontier, it has a strong impetus to ensure long-term stability. Second, Russia is also deeply concerned about both the causes and effects of Islamist-based terrorism, as it has already demonstrated elsewhere, both inside and outside its borders. Third, Russia has a significant interest in participating in economic projects, such as the development of Iraq's oil reserves.[5] Fourth, the West (including NATO) could benefit from having an added source of military forces, logistics capabilities, and experience in a number of civilian reconstruction areas.

A Russian role could also help to diffuse perceptions that the "West" was somehow seeking to impose its attitudes on Iraq and its people. Of course, such a role would depend much more on the actions both of the Iraqi interim government and of the external powers that retain forces in Iraq than on Russia. Yet Russia's involvement in the near future is quite important and includes maintaining and strengthening the global antiterrorist coalition.

NATO has not yet defined its role in Iraq. But if NATO were to decide to become more involved, NATO and Russia should consider participating in a joint civil-military operation in Iraq as the new government develops its mandate. This could take the form of special units in which NATO and Russia work together. The strategic and political objectives of these units could be to help Iraq establish a peaceful security environment and to begin the transition to practical sovereignty and political reform. Their joint operational objectives could include the following:

- assisting in monitoring Iraq's borders
- improving the capabilities and effectiveness of the national police, army, and other security forces
- assisting the UN (if present) with force protection and situational awareness
- helping in general reconstruction efforts.

Much like NATO-Russian cooperation until 2003 in SFOR in Bosnia and KFOR in Kosovo, the Russian political and military delegations at NATO Headquarters, along with their SHAPE counterparts, would need to do the following:

- develop special command and control arrangements for Russian forces (perhaps using the Deputy to SACEUR for Russian Forces)

---

[5] Lukoil, for example, signed a contract to supply gasoline and diesel fuel to Iraq.

- agree on a set of guiding principles that would govern NATO and Russian peacekeeping operations, including the civilian dimension
- identify the Russian sectors of responsibility (or joint responsibility)
- outline the fundamental military tasks for Russian forces
- establish a legal framework acceptable to all parties, perhaps including a Chapter VII UN Security Council mandate.

A joint NATO-Russia mission in Iraq would have several benefits. Most important, NATO and Russia share a desire for a stable and peaceful Iraq. This includes assisting in the creation of an Iraq that is both internally stable and peaceful toward its neighbors. Some form of Russian involvement should be welcome in a coalition that has included military personnel from such Eastern European and Central Asian countries as Ukraine, Kazakhstan, Hungary, Romania, Latvia, Lithuania, and Bulgaria.

NATO-Russia cooperation in Iraq would also involve several concerns. The first is that Russia will never put its forces under NATO's military command, at least as long as Russia is not a full participant in the Alliance's political decisionmaking. Since the NATO-Russia Council cannot replace the North Atlantic Council, that makes Russia's military engagement in Iraq quite unlikely, at least for the near term.

The second problem is that continuing instability in Iraq may undermine Moscow's willingness to send military forces. After all, a number of countries have refused to send their soldiers to Iraq or have withdrawn them after deployment because of the deteriorating security environment. It is also not totally clear whether NATO and Russia share complementary long-term strategic interests in Iraq beyond the desire for internal stability. They were competitors in the Middle East before and during the Cold War, and their policies have since then sometimes still been in conflict. Other potential obstacles include language barriers (especially Russian command of English), a Status-of-Forces-Agreement (SOFA) agreement, and interoperability of equipment and systems.

Iraq could probably become a central topic for consideration within the NATO-Russia Council. Discussions should include political issues, strategic assessments, coordination of policy, and the full range of appropriate activities related to possible cooperation in Iraq. This could also become an opportunity for associating Russia with NRF, if it is assigned a role in Iraq.

Cooperation in Central Asia and the Transcaucasus

Central Asia and the Transcaucasus are also potential areas for NATO-Russian cooperation, in the future, in the contexts of both the NATO-Russia Council and the Euro-Atlantic Partnership Council. These are, however, also areas in which potential conflicts of interest and policy may arise that will need to be dealt with effectively. In recent years, NATO has intensified cooperation with the countries of Central Asia and the Transcaucasus through PFP, while Russia has sought to give the Collective Security Treaty Organization (CSTO) a stronger military and antiterrorist component.[6]

---

[6] Russia has also established an antiterrorism center in Tashkent under the rubric of the CSTO.

Moreover, both Russia and NATO share an interest in dampening regional conflicts and combating terrorism in Central Asia and the Transcaucasus. One possibility worth exploring would be for NATO and Russia to conduct joint peacekeeping missions, preferably under a UN mandate.

It has to be recognized that many in Russia are very suspicious about NATO's growing military involvement in the former Soviet republics near Russia's borders. But this concern may ease, assuming that Russia and NATO forge a truly cooperative relationship. If this happens, we may expect a new range of possibilities for joint action.

For instance, NATO and Russia could form a joint peacekeeping unit to monitor a (future) settlement of the Nagorno-Karabakh conflict or to conduct joint border protection in Tajikistan or Georgia, if that proved feasible in either situation. In the case of Nagorno-Karabakh, this could involve supervising the withdrawal and containment of military forces, following a settlement, as well as ensuring that both sides abide by the agreement.[7] At the same time, both Russia and NATO—as well as regional countries—could benefit from keeping the Organisation for Security and Cooperation in Europe (OSCE) engaged. Properly done, this can both meet a Russian political preference and not interfere with NATO's sense of primacy.

NATO and Russia, along with states in the region, could also conduct joint exercises to combat terrorism in Central Asia. These could be conducted within the framework of either PFP or NRF. Such exercises could enhance stability in Central Asia and the Transcaucasus. At the same time, they could help build confidence in an area in which both Western countries and Russia have particular concerns about the interests and activities of the other but also share an overriding objective of not blundering into a new Great Game. Through such exercises, each side would become more closely acquainted with the military doctrine and training procedures of the other side. This could help reduce mistrust and suspicion on both sides and promote a spirit of greater cooperation and confidence.

Only a few years ago, such cooperation would have been unacceptable to either side. But the strong mutual interest in combating terrorism and in underpinning regional stability could make both sides more receptive. Moreover, Bosnia and Kosovo set precedents for peacekeeping or peace-monitoring operations in one or more parts of Central Asia and the Transcaucasus, as appropriate to all concerned, particularly the local parties.

However, even if the political will could be found, several technical obstacles to such cooperation currently exist. None of these would be an insurmountable obstacle if both sides agreed to make cooperation a priority. These include the following:

- *Language.* Most Russian officers lack sufficient command of English to allow them to communicate effectively with NATO forces. Thus, Russia would have to enhance its English-language training for officers.
- *Financing.* Russia has participated in PFP exercises only sporadically. Insufficient financing is a major problem for the Russian armed forces and significantly hinders their ability to operate effectively with non-Russian forces. Clearly, it is necessary to allocate sufficient resources for training and exercises in order for Russians to participate in joint exercises with NATO. NATO countries should be ready to help underwrite these activities, in accordance with Russian interests and desires.

---

[7] Indeed, the prospect of such a joint effort might be an added incentive for Armenia and Azerbaijan to reach a settlement.

- *Status of Forces Agreement.* NATO and Russia would need to negotiate a SOFA that would allow them to deploy troops and military equipment on each other's territory.

Israeli-Palestinian Peacekeeping

At the end of April 2003, the United States, Russia, the UN, and the EU—the so-called Quartet—published their road map for peacemaking between Israel and a prospective Palestinian state.[8] At the time this report was being prepared, the chances that the road map will be fulfilled are problematic. Nevertheless, at some point, peace negotiations may succeed and produce the two-state solution—an Israel and a Palestine living side by side in peace (at least nominally). It is almost certain that some outside help will be required to preserve security and to build confidence between the parties. Given the political views of the local parties, the United States would almost certainly have to be involved in a peacekeeping or "peace enabling" force. But U.S. involvement by itself may be not sufficient, and since the Iraq war, the United States might not have the necessary forces, depending on the situation in Iraq and elsewhere at the time.

That is why all parties, including the United States, would find merit in making this a NATO-led operation. In that context, there should be a role for Russia. This would reflect Russian interests, its role in the road map, and opportunities for practical cooperation between Russia and NATO in an area of deep and consuming interest to all concerned. Unlike the Soviet Union, Russia today enjoys a good deal of credibility, not only among Arabs but also among many people in Israel, where Russian immigrants are quite numerous.

The Working Group on NATO-Russia Relations thus recommends that the NATO-Russia Council, along with military bodies, begin considering the possibilities of such a development and, if it were to be pursued, the practical requirements for bringing it to fruition. Indeed, such an effort might, at some point, be an added spur to the success of negotiations between Israel and the Palestinians.

New Middle East Security System

Over the last several years, especially since the Iraq War, it has become increasingly clear that the Middle East, especially the Persian Gulf region, needs a new security system. All Western states and Russia have interests and concerns in this region, many of which have been presented above. One added interest they should share is for relations among the regional states to evolve enough that it will not always be necessary for outside forces and an outside presence to guarantee security. This would mean not just an absence of fighting but also the elimination of WMD, a reduction in terrorism (causes, activities, and consequences), and the progressive modernization and transformation of the region. The NATO-Russia cooperative efforts recommended above can be of use. Both the West and Russia would also benefit from

---

[8] See U.S. Department of State, "A Performance-Based Roadmap to a Permanent Two-State Solution to the Israeli-Palestinian Conflict," press statement, April 30, 2003; online at http://www.state.gov/r/pa/prs/ps/2003/20062.htm (as of September 23, 2004).

a new system of relations among regional states that would greatly reduce the need for outside military engagement and intervention.[9]

Such a system should be designed to replace the so-called dual containment policy of the United States, from 1992 onward, in which neither Iran nor Iraq was judged to be available as an effective partner for providing security in the region. That may become possible again because, for example, Russia has much better relations with Iran than does the United States (despite some remaining problems between Moscow and Teheran). Postconflict, postreconstruction Iraq might also be able to play such a role at some point. In any event, it would be useful for regional countries, NATO and Western countries, and Russia to begin exploring the possibility of some new structure and organization (which might resemble OSCE or another model, formal or informal, limited or comprehensive) to be developed over time—on an inclusive, nondiscriminatory basis. Among other places for such discussions to take place would be the NATO-Russia Council (including regional representation) and also the Euro-Atlantic Partnership Council.

---

[9] Until the Iranian Revolution of 1979, and to a degree until the Persian Gulf War of 1991, the United States, for its part, had generally practiced an "over the horizon" policy toward the Persian Gulf region: keeping land and air forces, plus major combatant vessels, largely out of sight, for political reasons, but near enough to be available if needed.

CHAPTER FOUR

The Future of Russia *Within* NATO

Since the beginning of NATO's post–Cold War transformation in the early 1990s and decisions, both in allied capitals and in Moscow, to develop a direct NATO-Russian relationship, the issue of the long-term nature of that relationship has been unclear. The Founding Act and the new NATO-Russia Council have helped, but they still do not point to a lasting relationship and its particular possibilities and requirements.

One school of thought within the Alliance argued that Russia should understand clearly at the outset that it would be unlikely ever to be asked to join NATO. This was not centrally about Russia's internal political and economic system and the possibilities of developing according to a "Western" model. That is quite possible and, indeed, could be seen as desirable for the Alliance in terms of lasting security in Europe. At heart, this view was shaped by the old suspicions related to Russia's traditional culture, its size relative to all the European members of NATO (individually and indeed collectively), and the enormous changes in the nature of the Alliance that Russian membership would entail. Of particular concern are the implications of extending the North Atlantic Treaty's Article 5 security provisions to a country whose territory extends so far from "Europe" (very few seem to realize that the United States is geographically far away from Europe) and that borders on so many other countries and areas of difficulty, including China. According to this school of thought, making clear to Russia that it would not be considered for NATO membership would enable both it and the Alliance to establish a long-term relationship on the basis of some basic understandings about their respective futures and about both the limits and possibilities of what they could expect to do together.

Some contemporary Russian thinking also reflects this view, not being able to imagine the Federation's being matched with much smaller countries, even though NATO membership does include the theoretical (but not practical) notion that each ally is equal, at least in that all are covered by Article 5 and are able to block North Atlantic Council decisions. Thus, in the early period of PFP, some Russian commentators argued against joining a program that would give Russia the same status as minor Central European states. This attitude was reinforced by the two waves of NATO's enlargement despite Russia's objections.

Another school of thought within NATO argued that, while it was most unlikely that either NATO or Russia would ultimately agree to Russian membership, the notion of "equal opportunity" to join should be preserved. This view was based on the desire not to see the continent "redivided" between the countries that could join Western institutions and those that could not. This was also seen as an important message to send to Russians who were discomfited—for psychological as much as for any lingering security reasons—by the enlargement of NATO membership to include countries in Central Europe and even parts of the former Soviet Union. The goal of a "Europe whole and free" should also include the idea that all countries are eligible to join any of Europe's institutions and to take part in any of its other arrangements, formal and informal.

For its part, some Russians embraced this view, for a similar reason: underscoring that Russia should not appear to be the perennial pariah in Europe's family. That would make Russia subject to lasting discrimination from the outset, however little-prized inclusion might be and whatever other considerations there might be about various forms of relationship with the West. But nowadays, there is no serious discussion in Russia about full membership in NATO.

A third school of thought, more evident in some Russian thinking than in NATO capitals, has suggested the possibility of some form of associate membership, but many observers in both Russia and NATO doubt that there is much to distinguish between such a relationship and what already exists. NATO has always resisted the notion of a half-way house, which lacks the precision of the various forms of engagement with NATO, its mutual and reciprocal commitments, and its institutions and their processes.

Finally, there has indeed been a school of thought that foresees the possibility of practical, relatively near-term full membership for Russia in NATO. But in the West, this view has been restricted largely to people who see the Alliance as something like the Organization for Security and Cooperation in Europe (OSCE). If it is, why have two institutions with similar purposes and memberships? In Russia, proponents of this view have generally been those who want NATO to become a political and security association instead of an alliance with military structures and responsibilities.

The debate, such as it is, has rested thus for several years. Thirteen years after the dissolution of the Soviet Union, seven years after the formalization of direct NATO-Russia relations following the Founding Act, and with the radical changes in the geopolitics of European security, the Working Group on NATO-Russia relations believes it is time to revisit the basic question of Russia's long-term engagement with NATO.

This does not mean that the Working Group is recommending that Russia be invited to join NATO today—or that Russia should seek such an invitation. If that became mutually desirable, advantageous, and practicable, the nature of global politics would likely have changed enough to have radically redefined *NATO*.

Instead, the working group suggests further developing the idea of a deeply engaged role for Russia in deliberations about the future of areas contiguous to it, as well as in matters that can generally be gathered under the heading of "globalization." Russia's membership in the Group of Eight, while not always on a truly equal basis with all its members in terms of such factors as gross domestic product (not all of the original Group of Seven pass that threshold), is evidence of this development. Indeed, in the long-term effort to shape a world that is less likely to produce conflict (including international terrorism), the nonmilitary cooperation of all advanced societies is an opportunity and perhaps also a necessity. Within the Group of Eight, Russia is much more important than some of other members with much bigger gross domestic products.

The objectives in NATO-Russia relations, as they move forward, should be to

- solidify the practical bases for day-to-day NATO-Russia cooperation, engaging the full range of government structures and domestic political processes (to make the interactions more institutionalized and diversified)

- work toward a true sense of "equality" in NATO-Russia activities, even when neither Russia nor NATO is entirely within one another's decisionmaking structures, with each respecting the areas in which the other must retain a capacity for separate deliberation and even independence of action; even within the Alliance, allies have similarity but not identity of interests
- ensure that what they do together also preserves the interests of third parties with which they are associated, including members of the Euro-Atlantic Partnership Council (without allowing some old and perhaps historically justified suspicions to block progress)
- seize on opportunities to build confidence, at all levels, and progressively look toward common actions where compatible interests are involved; this would include parallel consideration of issues within the NATO framework at three levels (the North Atlantic Council, the NATO-Russia Council, and the Euro-Atlantic Partnership Council), with transparent support structures
- broaden NATO-Russia cooperation to include relevant and appropriate EU cooperation
- intensify personnel exchanges and educational opportunities at all levels
- promote complementarity of and cooperation in nonofficial relationships, including the private sector, and increasing engagement of Russians in nongovernmental organizations (NGOs).

At heart, the NATO-Russia relationship will be about what NATO and Russia do together, acknowledging that they share a wide-ranging complementarity of interests. Building on that complementarity can further aid the development of a truly equal, mutually supportive relationship that can help bring to fruition the goal of a "Europe whole and free"—indeed, a goal encompassing areas well beyond Europe. In pursuit of this goal, both NATO and Russia should share responsibilities, and each should behave responsibly toward the other.

RAND-ISKRAN Working Group on NATO-Russia Relations

Cochairs

Ambassador Robert Hunter, Senior Advisor, RAND
Dr. Sergey Rogov, Director, Institute for USA and Canada Studies

Russian Members

Svetlana Babich, Institute of USA and Canada Studies
Dr. Vladimir Baranovsky, Institute of World Economy and International Relations
Colonel-General Victor Esin (retired), First Vice-President, Academy for Security, Defense, Law and Order Studies
Dr. Edward Ivanyan, Department Head, Institute of USA and Canada Studies
Dr. Vladimir Lukin, Vice-Chairman of the State Duma of the Russian Federation
Dr. Irina Modnikova, Institute of USA and Canada Studies
Dr. Mikhail Nosov, First Deputy Director, Institute for USA and Canada Studies
Dr. Natalya Osipova, Senior Research Fellow, Institute for USA and Canada Studies
Dr. Mikhail Portnoy, Department Head, Institute of USA and Canada Studies
Major General Vladimir Sizov (retired), Academy of the General Staff
Dr. Nikolay Shmelev, Director of the Institute of Europe
Dr. Alexander Shumilin, Director for the Center for the Study of the Greater Middle East Conflict, Institute for USA and Canada Studies
Dr. Inna Sokolova, Institute of USA and Canada Studies
Dr. Victor Supyan, Deputy Director, Institute of USA and Canada Studies
Dr. Viltaliy Zhurkin, Director Emeritus of the Institute of Europe, Russian Academy of Sciences
Lieutenant-General Nikolay Zlenko (retired), Head of Advisory board of the "Vnesheconombank"
Major-General Pavel Zolotarev (retired), President, Foundation for Military Reform

European Members

Alyson J. K. Bailes, Director, Stockholm International Peace Research Institute
Brig. General Dieter Farwick (retired), Global Editor-in-Chief, World Security Network
Dr. Hubertus Hoffman, President, World Security Network

Dr. Janusz Onyzkiewicz, Center of International Relations, Warsaw, and former Polish Minister of Defense.
Stefano Silvestri, President, *Istituto Affari Internazionali*

U.S. Members

Dr. Stephen Larrabee, Corporate Chair, European Security, RAND (project codirector)
Ambassador James F. Collins, Senior International Advisor, Akin Gump Strauss Hauer & Feld, Former Ambassador of the United States to the Russian Federation,
Ambassador James Dobbins, Director, International Security and Defense Policy Center, RAND Corporation
Dr. Stephen J. Flanagan, Director, Institute for National Strategic Studies, National Defense University
Paul Fritch, Head of Section, Russia and Ukraine Relations, Political Affairs Division, NATO Headquarters
Leon Fuerth, Research Professor, Elliott School of International Affairs, George Washington University
Dr. Henry Gaffney, Director, Strategy and Concepts Group, The CNA Corporation
Dr. Michael Haltzel, Senior Professional Staff Member, Senate Foreign Relations Committee
Scott A. Harris, President, Lockheed Martin Continental Europe
Dr. Seth Jones, Policy Analyst, RAND Corporation (rapporteur)
C. William Maynes, President, The Eurasia Foundation
Robert J. Murray, President and CEO, the CNA Corporation
Olga Oliker, International Policy Analyst, RAND (rapporteur)
Dr. John Peters, Senior Researcher, RAND Corporation
Vice Admiral Norman W. Ray, USN (retired), President, Raytheon International
William H. Siefken, Director, International Business Development, Lockheed Martin
David C. Speedie, Special Advisor to the President and Director, Islam Project, Carnegie Corporation
Dr. James A. Thomson, President and Chief Executive Officer, RAND Corporation
Ted Warner, Vice President, Booz Allen-Hamilton

Canadian Member

Dr. Joel J. Sokolsky, Dean of Arts and Professor of Political Science, Royal Military College of Canada.

APPENDIX B

The NATO-Russia Dialogue: An (Unrepentantly) European View

Alyson J. K. Bailes[1]

As a believer in the European Union (EU) and also in its security vocation—a belief shared by a surprising number of people out in the real world[2]—I would like to suggest that the best service we can do for NATO and the NATO-Russian dialogue is to place them in proper perspective within a wider strategic reality. The NATO-Russian relationship has a special and irreplaceable role to play in this picture and must play it to the full. But we shall only hurt both NATO and Russia by placing upon their relationship a burden that it was not designed for and cannot bear.

For the last fifty years, it has generally been true both that NATO embodied Russia's main problem in relations with the West and that NATO had it in its power to offer Russia the solution (or at least a palliative) for this problem:

- In the Cold War, NATO could destroy Russia and vice versa, but NATO and Russia also engaged very actively (through arms control negotiations[3]) to find a way to avoid doing that, and found a solution that helped to keep the peace both during the Cold War and during the transition out of it.
- In the 1990s, NATO led the way in enlargement, going both faster and wider than the EU; it also helped to solve the related problems for Russia (though the solution is clearly not yet complete or completely accepted) by transparency, voluntary limitations on the nature of its presence on new members' territory, letting Russia into its current operations, and strengthening the institutional relationship between Russia itself and NATO's decisionmaking bodies.

The new strategic environment since the start of the 21st century is being shaped by a number of trends that reduce the centrality, or at least relativize the importance, of this historic relationship. In simplified terms and not necessary in any order of priority, they include

- the new salience of threats from transnational terrorism, WMD proliferation, and the failed states and rogue states who engage in or abet them;

---

[1] Director of the Stockholm International Peace Research Institute.

[2] The opinion poll "Transatlantic Trends 2003." sponsored by the German Marshall Center. found in autumn 2003 that 80 percent of U.S. respondents wanted to see stronger EU leadership, and 37 percent even approved of the proposition that the EU would become a superpower. Opinion polls within Europe also show that the level of approval for CFSP is not significantly lower among the new entrant countries than in "old" Europe.

[3] Which possibly took up more man-hours than the positive NATO-Russian engagement now, especially since Russian troops have left the Balkan operations.

- the nature of the U.S. response, which was initially to disavow institutional and legal constraints ("the mission makes the coalition," preemption without UN authority) and to play down the value of traditional partnerships with both Europe and Russia[4]
- the shaky but steady rise of the EU as a conscious security actor, including the EU's own expansion up to Russia's borders with all its consequences for mutual friction, engagement, and interdependence[5]
- new patterns of penetration and mutual dependence in the global economy and energy market, in which Russia's engagement is deepening as a consequence (*inter alia*) of new property laws and an improving investment security rating within Russia itself and of the increasing motive for Western users to explore non-Arab sources of energy.

The net effect of these forces so far has been to create both new tensions and new openings in the U.S.-Europe-Russia strategic triangle. During 2002–2003, the U.S. sometimes found a readier understanding for its concerns and a more pragmatic partnership response in Moscow than in many European capitals. Russia discovered ways to use the "new threats" agenda for promoting its national interests (e.g., by lessening international oversight and criticism of Russian actions in Chechnya). At other times Germany, France, and Russia lined up together against the U.S., United Kingdom, and other western European players (and over the heads of the "new Europeans"). By autumn 2003, the fruits of these diverse and divisive maneuvers were clearly starting to taste more bitter than sweet for all concerned, and political energies were turned back into bridge-building efforts between the U.S. and Europe, between Europeans, and also—though seemingly as a second-order priority— between Washington and Moscow. The important point for the present argument, however, is that *neither this set of splits nor the initial "deals" that helped resolve them passed through the Atlantic Alliance*. The Iraq crisis was not "about" NATO and was not NATO's fault. It affected NATO, rather, through its backwash and by the way it reinforced earlier opinions about the Alliance's reduced strategic relevance.[6] The bridge-building regarding the future handling of Iraq has—correspondingly—thus far proceeded mainly at the UN, in various economic and functional fora, and on nation-to-nation channels.[7]

As seen from the perspective of early 2004, the NATO-Russia relationship thus finds itself in a triple bind:

---

[4] As seen from the vantage point of early 2004, considerable movement has taken place back toward a U.S.-European and even a degree of U.S.-Russian consensus on where to go next in specific cases, such as Afghanistan and Iraq. The U.S. is also making much more constructive use of institutional possibilities, both in the UN and NATO, for tackling these and other broader agendas. However, it can still not be said that NATO, as such, has reclaimed the role of an *initiating* and *defining* institution for the U.S. national, or Euro-Atlantic, policy approaches to "new threat" situations. If anything, the UN may have a greater chance of reasserting its centrality, depending on the outcome of the "Group of Eminent Persons" reflection exercise set in hand by the UN Secretary-General and the attitude of the next U.S. President (from whichever party). See the arguments further on in the text.

[5] The greatest length of Russia's western frontier, through Finland down to the Baltic states, will from 2004 be an EU frontier and administered by EU rules (an EU "common border guard" is even under discussion). The short Norwegian-Russian border is now the only NATO-Russia one and is also run by EU rules to the extent that Norway is within the EU "Schengen" area. It was the EU, not NATO, and Russia who had to tackle the issue of the impact of enlargement on Kaliningrad.

[6] Arising notably from the fact that NATO's invocation of Article 5 in support of the U.S. on 12 September 2001 was never followed up in practice.

[7] Since the end of 2003, there has been growing speculation about a future NATO peacekeeping role in Iraq; however, and typically, this continues to be canvassed and prepared through essentially political and informal channels.

a. Many of the areas now opening up for *constructive* U.S.-Russian or U.S.-Europe-Russian interaction lie outside NATO's competence: energy, the economy (including that very great majority of defense industry and technology transactions that are determined by the private sector itself[8]), antiterrorist measures on the broader Europe's own territory (an EU matter), defense against nonmilitary threats (SARS, etc.), the "greater Middle East," cooperative action against Iranian and North Korean WMD, the general development of strategic export controls, global CBW disarmament, the "Proliferation Security Initiative" on sea transport of WMD, and even the task of destroying leftover WMD on Russia's own territory—now masterminded by the G-8's "Global Partnership" program with a major financial pledge from the EU.

b. Many of the things that Russia still *worries* about in U.S. (and to a much lesser extent, European) policies cannot be fixed by or even meaningfully discussed through NATO (though that will not stop Russia from trying). Examples include U.S. *national* policy on missile defense, U.S. *national* decisions about military intervention and basing policy (notably in Central Asia and potentially in southeast Europe), U.S. unilateral withdrawal from or refusal of (global and general) arms control constraints, the development of new conventional and nonconventional defense technologies in the U.S. and elsewhere, U.S. *national* restrictions on defense imports, industrial collaboration and technology transfer, and so forth.[9] The same self-evidently applies to Russian worries about the impact of EU enlargement, such as the many still-unresolved visa and travel questions and national and collective trade arrangements.

c. To give the final negative tilt to the balance, the most prominent actions being taken by NATO today in order to fulfill its existing agenda *and* help rebuild U.S.-European bridges in the defense dimension—the rather belated and muddled sorting-out of such enlargement consequences as Baltic air defense, the revived CFE controversy, the further extension of a NATO military role in Afghanistan, NATO practical support to some individual Allies engaged in Iraq, and the latest speculation about a collective follow-on role for NATO there—are of a nature to create *additional problems or at least new challenges and doubts* for Russia.[10]

In this complicated and still volatile situation, the single most important prescription for the success and survival of the NATO-Russia relationship is that it should be correctly viewed as *one strand and one tool* within a wider set of strategic interactions and should be

---

[8] The EU decided in November 2003 to prepare for setting up its own armaments- and capability-related agency, which will doubtless draw Russian attention.

[9] Many Europeans, as well as Russians, would *like* NATO to be able to discipline the U.S. on these issues, but trying to achieve that, especially with any appearance of Europe and Russia ganging up on the U.S., would, in present circumstances, merely test the U.S.'s now somewhat fragile tolerance of existing Alliance disciplines to the point of destruction.

[10] This text does not, at present, attempt to deal with a fourth factor that many observers would currently want to add to the picture, i.e., the risk or likelihood of more self-assertive Russian behavior after the imminent Presidential elections, in the sphere of European security as in others. In the past, the effect of such "frost" upon the West-Russia relationship has often been to make NATO more important as the guarantor of a Western common front and protector for its more exposed members, or the most tough and qualified Western negotiator for finding solutions to the tensions, or both. However, in present conditions, (a) how President Putin will want and will be able to act in reality, (b) whether the style-setting Western actors will find a sharpening of tension welcome or inconvenient, and (c) what role they will see NATO as playing in their strategies in either event are still very open questions. Whatever happens, it is already clear that the EU will also be an addressee for any changed Russian tactics and a key actor in responding to them, to a much greater degree than in the past.

given tasks and aims that are neither too large nor too small in this perspective. To put the challenge an other way: We face a situation today in which NATO's range of competence has proportionately narrowed, while Russia's appetite for engagement in previously West-dominated or intra-Western processes has grown. Western actors need to pay more attention than most of them have done so far to the second fact, and they need to develop a much-more-coherent vision than so far of how to use the NATO-Russia channel *among others* to guide Russia-West interactions in a direction meaningful and profitable for both parties.

From this starting point, three more specific guidelines for the NATO-Russia process may be proposed.

First, the least that can be expected from NATO is that it should take responsibility within the framework of this relationship for the things it is doing and has competence for, particularly those that fall within category (c) above. It should do more (even if this aim has already exhausted the patience of several saints) to achieve real Russia-West military dialogue and cooperation (and, in this context, should reflect on how Russia may gain or lose from proposed changes in PFP and knock-on effects in the EAPC). It should do more to find collaborative approaches for cleaning up the remaining debris of the Cold War, in Europe and possibly beyond, especially in areas *not* covered by the Global Partnership.[11] It should soldier on in trying to overcome the remaining obstacles to the entry into force, and extension to all new NATO members, of the Adapted CFE Treaty.[12] It should plug away at the issue of substrategic nuclear weapons, the most yawning hole in NATO's and Russia's joint arms control inheritance from the Cold War. It should cover the aspects of missile defense development on which NATO *has* been brought into the picture on the Western side.

Most urgent of all, people on both sides of the dialogue need to think about how to turn NATO's new ambitions for outreach into the West Asian–Middle Eastern "arc of crisis" from a spanner in the NATO-Russia works into a new source of fuel for the process. Countries other than Russia would clearly like to know what the limits of NATO's relevance are in this process and what the ultimate logic of NATO's engagement will be, for the region as well as for Afghanistan and Iraq themselves. The most foolish answers, the attempted creation of isolated Western puppet states (based ultimately on the arbitrary logic of whom we chose to invade lately) and/or the imposition of an artificial regional organizing framework from outside, would be particularly disturbing for Russia but also inappropriate and foolhardy for NATO itself. There is an intermediate solution—the establishment of new spheres of influence, with the West policing a line from Iraq to Afghanistan and Russia policing the frontiers of its CIS neighbors—that looks at first glance like a good bargain for Russia but may overstretch both sides' capability in practice, as well as being an objectionable "neo-Yalta" approach in principle.

The remaining range of good solutions, based on consolidation of a regional peace order respecting national sovereignties and on the complementary use of several institutions including those where Russia has a vote,[13] still remains to be worked out but should not

---

[11] See "Relics of Cold War: Europe's Challenge, Ukraine's Experience," SIPRI Policy Paper 6, November 2003, available at http://www.sipri.org). See also the research report to be published by Ian Anthony through SIPFWOUP later in Spring 2004, offering a constructive critique of the achievements of Cooperative Threat Reduction and the problems and limitations of Global Partnership.

[12] This is an issue on which real mutual leverage and hence the prospect of a really meaningful trade-off does exist between the two sides in a NATO framework, which would be lost through any attempt to break out of that framework.

[13] Such as the UN, G-8, and possibly OSCE.

include any alternative that either undermines Russia or provokes Russia to undermine it.[14] The problem is that, in finding the mutually acceptable answers, both Russia and the West start out with substantially worse cards in their hands than they held in the—itself extremely difficult—case of the Balkan wars. There are few if any local constituencies in the "arc of crisis" with reason to welcome (as the Serbs did) the addition of Russia to Western intervening forces and Western reconstruction strategies. The West, for its part, does not know or in any complete sense control the terrain; has to work with "front-line states" (such as Syria, Iran and Pakistan) that are part of the problem, compared with (say) Hungary or Greece in the Balkans; and cannot use the prospect of European integration (or any credible local alternative) for leverage and inspiration. Oil provides a whole cross-cutting agenda in which there are no short cuts to reconciling Western, Russian, and local interests. However tough it might seem, talking out some of these problems in the presence of Russian ears and voices might offer better results (as well as less damage) than setting up either a quick fix or an insubstantial whitewash job for the region behind Russia's back.

Second, a special effort will be needed in this phase to avoid letting issues outside NATO's competence and control poison the NATO-Russian dialogue. In the 1990s, when Russia temporarily withdrew from cooperation in Partnership for Peace, it was at least in response to something (enlargement plans) that NATO was actually doing. It would be a double pity to repeat such total or partial blockages today for essentially extrinsic reasons.[15] This does not mean that Russia should not be free to *raise* such concerns and use the NATO-Russian channel to raise Western consciousness of them—as the Western side could also consider doing in reverse, when merited. But operational linkages and horse-trading between issues inside and outside NATO's own agenda, however tempting they may seem at the time, should be avoided like the plague. Making this work will obviously be easier if the dialogue contains a continuous ballast of "happy" topics and activities to balance the occasional harsh words. If some further degree of formalization, regularization, and institutionalization of the dialogue could be achieved during this period, it would have a value in itself insofar (and only insofar) as it might raise the threshold against ill-thought-through "walk-out" tactics.

The last and largest point is that Russia needs to recapture some of the strategic wisdom that always—however counterintuitive, and usually unspoken—underlay its crucial decisions in the Cold War period regarding the value of keeping the U.S. strategically engaged in Europe. The arguments why this is in Russia's ultimate interest hold just as good in 21st-century circumstances as they ever did. If anything, Russia would have even more to lose now from a renationalization of Western European defense, from the escalation of Balkans-type conflicts in its Western back yard, or from a situation where the only neigh-

---

[14] In the author's view, though this is not a fashionable argument, it should also take account of the lessons (including some positive ones) of Russia's own engagement in regional multilateral security processes, notably the Shanghai Cooperation Organization, which has achieved confidence-building measures and common new threat programmes between Russia, China, and four Central Asian states. See the chapter by D. Trofimov in "Armament and Disarmament in the Caucasus and Central Asia," SIPRI Policy Paper no. 3, July 2003, online at http://www.sipri.org, and the paper on the SCO at the same web address by Chinese author Ren Dongfeng.

[15] The danger is particularly great in a phase when Russia is making complaints to the EU and NATO in parallel about the same countries engaged in two parallel and synchronous enlargement processes and when the EU is still demonstrably inexperienced and sometimes amateurish in its Russia-handling strategy. Letting Russia play the two institutions against each other, or letting it prevail on actors in one institution to precook a decision to be taken in the other, would be fatal not just for Western interests but for healthy Russian relations with both institutions in the longer run.

boring Western organization it has to negotiate with is the EU.[16] It also has (whether it admits it or lot) much less to lose from an efficient NATO now that the Alliance has *de facto* switched its whole operational focus away from the old agenda of collective territorial defense. With the consummation of this agenda shift, the present enlargement, and the further range of countries (such as the Western Balkans) holding a promise of ultimate EU membership, the functional parallel between the U.S. and Russian roles as "semi-integrated," but defining presences in the European strategic space has become even clearer.

Third, and most obviously, the lessons of 2001–2003 about what a *disengaged*, Alliance-free, unilateralist, and self-targeting U.S. would mean should have been just as frightening or even more frightening for Russians than they have been for any European.

How do these lofty considerations relate to the NATO-Russian dialogue? The current U.S.-European and inter-European bridge-building impulses referred to above have not entirely bypassed NATO. They have included very deliberate efforts, not least from Paris, to repair the political fabric of the Alliance and to find it new tasks capable of providing, at least, good occupational therapy for some time to come. Even the most cynical and the most idealistic Europeans have understood that the fragile disciplines of the Alliance offer the best and (for the moment) the only hold we can claim over the U.S., as a potential sole superpower in the security dimension, and also that, if the U.S. is ready to start walking back into multilateralist rule-based cooperation after the lessons of Iraq, its shortest walk is into the doors of NATO. It does not require a particularly developed taste for paradox to see that keeping NATO alive, credible, and *interesting* to the U.S. for these purposes can be in Russia's best interest as well. Could wise heads in Moscow make the same transition as at least some wise heads have made in Paris, from seeing NATO mechanisms as a U.S.-owned trap for themselves to seeing them as a trap that they might (in the nicest possible way) help to close upon the U.S.? Adoption of such a strategy, let alone success in it, might do more to salvage NATO's relative importance both in itself and for Russia-West interaction than could any of the more particular recipes discussed above.

---

[16] This may seem a paradoxical remark. But Russia's self-image and self-respect, since the fall of the USSR in particular, demand the existence of at least some framework in which it is seen as an equal and in some sense "balancing" partner to the West. This is (still) more the case in NATO, and in U.S.-Russian strategic dialogue, where the focus is on nuclear and other military realities than it is in Russia-EU relations, in which Russia falls so far below the standards in which EU core strengths and EU obligations are measured. It is much more natural for the EU than for NATO to see Russia as "just another country"—and indeed, as the least (ultimately) "integratable" of its neighbors. No wonder that Russia has always tried to build up the *strategic* elements in EU-Russia dialogue.

NATO-Russia Military Cooperation

Dieter Farwick[1]

This report is designed to help the NATO-Russia Council (NRC) improve military cooperation between NATO and the Russian Federation in the area of training and exercises. It follows a bottom-up approach, which has the merit of helping to avoid political sensitivities.

In response to NRC guidance, NATO's strategic commanders—the Supreme Allied Commander Europe (SACEUR) and the Supreme Allied Commander Transformation (SACT)—developed an education and training program together with the Main Operations Directorate of the Russian General Staff. Thus, many activities are currently being conducted in the field of military cooperation, at all three levels of NATO—political, strategic, and operational—in close cooperation within the NRC, as well as between NATO headquarters and the Main Operations Directorate. Under the label "Russia Interoperability Framework Activities," for 2004, more than 40 activities have been agreed upon. These include seminars, language training, and lectures for a limited number of individuals.

The key word is *interoperability*. Under this label, communications at the tactical, operational, and strategic levels have been assigned first priority. With joint operations as the long-term objective, it has been decided to choose a step-by-step approach, because there are no preconditions for joint and combined operations on the Russian side. At the same time, another aim was to avoid activities with political implications or sensitivities. The program has been developed by military operators—not by diplomats or politicians in uniform. These soldiers from both sides—NATO and Russia—defined the topics. Thus activities of all three services in 2004 include the following:

- a sea-based exercise in the Baltic Sea to exercise "naval communications interoperability"
- a higher commanders' training workshop, with two Russian generals taking part with NATO counterparts
- a workshop on Commonwealth of Independent States (CIS) interoperability with NATO forces, conducted at AFSOUTH, including five Russian technical specialists from Main Operations Directorate
- a Combined Joint Task Force (CJTF)workshop at AFNORTH, with up to seven Russian officers
- "Cooperative Best Effort," a squad-level Live Exercise (Livex)

---

[1] Brigadier General (retired) Dieter Farwick, German Army, has extensive NATO and national expertise in training and exercises. For several years, he was Chief of Operations at NATO-Headquarters AFCENT (today: AFNORTH). This report is based upon studies on current NRC activities and future opportunities, including study of NATO documents and interviews with various NATO officials at all levels at the International Military Staff, NATO Headquarters (Brussels), SHAPE (Mons, Belgium) and AFNORTH (Brunssum, Netherlands).

- an Air Transport Seminar in Russia, concentrating on communication and coordination concepts of NATO Air Transport Operations.

It is obvious that these activities are aimed primarily at individuals and at the unit and subunit levels. It is a kind of cadre training and formation. There is also a permanent evaluation and planning process, coordinated by NATO Headquarters and the Russian Main Operations Directorate, that will evaluate, on a yearly basis, the current program and will design future programs based on the lessons learned.

This kind of "cadre development" will go on at least until 2006. In addition, there are activities to exploit common lessons learned from SFOR and KFOR.

Overall, therefore, the program "Russia Interoperability Framework Activities," which brings operators together, is already a success story and generally on a good path. There is no need for micromanagement from higher levels. But there is a need for political support. This is particularly true in regard to three stumbling blocks, two major and one minor: English language training, budgeting, and the missing SOFA. The last-named is a political issue between NATO and the Russian federation, but its resolution is a prerequisite for the exchange of individuals and troops.

Regarding language training, it goes without saying that no Russian general or officer can work in a NATO joint headquarters without sufficient language skills. Working with a lot of interpreters is not practical and is too expensive.

Many Russian officers have taken part in English-language courses, both with NATO and NATO nations. The host nations have invested scarce resources, but the effect has been limited. Language-trained officers did not come back into the "military cooperation business," where they could have improved their language skills and brought in their professional skills. Thus, with low language skills and interpreters, the effect of any cooperation remains limited. The cost-benefit relations are poor. As a result, the Russian side needs to improve personnel management in order to ensure that the right people get English-language training, with a follow-up commitment in the area of NATO-Russia cooperation. This is the only way to "produce" generals and officers who can be brought into a program of jointness and integration.

The second problem is money. All activities could integrate more Russian generals and officers than in 2004, if the resources were available. NATO, NATO nations, and Russia should all find means to solve this problem. Indeed, the best-suited framework for further Russian integration with NATO activities is the Partnership for Peace (PFP)program, but it needs much more money. Russia, unfortunately, missed about ten years of the PFP program, in which generals and officers from other non-NATO-members have been brought up to NATO standards. These other non-NATO members of the program have been drawing benefits from participation in all kinds of activities, leading to development of capabilities to participate in PFP joint and combined exercises, based upon the CJTF concept. They are now able to take part in joint and combined operations. The same now needs to be done with Russian forces. In NATO, the Allied Command for Transformation (ACT)" in Norfolk, Virginia, has the lead in this program, with the Main Operations Directorate as counterpart. In this program, the NATO School at Oberammergau plays an important role, offering various courses. In addition, there are Mobile Education Teams to be sent to various academies in Russia.

Following proper training, Russian officers should be fully integrated into one or more of NATO's CJTF headquarters that are conducting joint and combined peace support operations. This capacity for direct and full engagement within NATO exercises and operations should also be the desired goal for Russian generals and officers. But there is a long way to go. Bringing Russian officers up to basic PFP standards would probably take to the end of 2006.

If the Russians and the NRC now intend to have Russian generals and officers participating inside NATO-led headquarters in command and control of joint and combined peace support operations, it will be necessary for the Russian military to end its reluctance to take part in practical terms within the PFP program.

Another long-term issue is the Russian relationship to NRF, since it is designed to play a role in both Article 5 and peace support operations. For the next few years, however, non-NATO members are likely to be excluded from NRF exercises and, so far, Russian participation is not part of the NRF concept. But this exclusion should not continue forever. Indeed, NATO and PFP exercises will increasingly concentrate on training and exercising the NRF. Beyond 2010—if not sooner—ways should be found to integrate Russian and other non-NATO forces in NRF peace support exercises and operations. There might be scenarios in which joint and combined peace support operations open to non-NATO countries would be conducted instead of just limiting operations to "NRF-NATO only."

NRC should give clear guidance and direction, as well as support, to NATO Strategic Commanders and the Russian General Staff in order to develop the ambitious program "beyond 2006." The ultimate goal of the overall NATO-Russia military cooperation program has been well defined by NATO Strategic Commanders and the Russian General Staff. Capabilities have to be built and maintained that would enable Russian generals, staff officers, and troops to operate within a CJTF during NATO-led non-Article 5 operations. Looking ahead, however, one should not mix "interoperability" between forces and "integration" of generals and staff officers in NATO-led CJTF Headquarters.

Another issue is that of the division of labor between the NATO Headquarters and NATO nations. It may come as a surprise to outsiders that interoperability between forces of different countries is not a particularly difficult problem, if it is kept at the right level. Thus, as the experience of ground forces has shown, a battalion is the lowest-level formation that could be integrated into a multinational brigade. NATO has been doing this for decades. For a limited period of time, a battalion with its own organic logistic elements can be integrated into a brigade of another nation. Even better would be a brigade that would be integrated into a multinational division.

In the past, NATO's Article 5 exercises, beginning in the 1960s and extending to actual peace support operations in the Balkans, have reflected this type of integration. In Kosovo, for example, a Russian battalion was made part of a German brigade, and the arrangement worked. It is primarily a question of mission definition and liaison. The battalion headquarters—especially the commander—must be able to take orders from the brigade headquarters and report, as well as keep in contact with its neighbors. That can be done by liaison teams that speak the language of the brigade or English, which normally will be the official common language. Within the battalion, the language is national. It would be good to have more officers and noncommissioned officers speaking English, but that is not a requirement. Orders and rules of engagement can be can be translated into the respective languages.

One should not overburden non-NATO nations, however. Even in NATO forces, language skills at the unit and subunit levels are poor. Integrating individual generals and staff officers into a NATO-led CJTF headquarters is a much more difficult task. It will take quite some time to get there. Because there is no room for interpreters, the individual general and staff officer must be able to do his or her job in English—not with an Oxford diploma but with sufficient skills. That is the prerequisite for working on a computer and for working within a team with members from different countries. The person has to be able to give clear orders and to understand even complicated messages. He or she has to communicate with superior and subordinate commands. He or she has to brief about his or her area of responsibility. He or she has to understand NATO's CJTF headquarters concepts, NATO and PFP standard operating procedures, job descriptions, and planning procedures. Likewise, generals and higher staff officers will have to work with media and indigenous representatives, for example, in the area of civil and military cooperation (CIMIC).

That desired end state can be achieved through individual training, workshops, and seminars, leading to CJTF headquarters command-post exercises, as the final step. These command-post exercises, with repeated commitments of individuals, will bring the participants up to NATO standards.

Prior to a real-world deployment, there must be a command-post exercise or mission rehearsal exercise to train the people who will be sent into an operation. At the end of the exercise, the operational capabilities have to be certified by the so-called "mounting headquarters." NATO headquarters did this in the past prior to real-world commitments, and they will also do it with Russian participants.

The way to this end state has to be directed and orchestrated by NATO headquarters and NATO nations. The former should stick to its level of command and expertise—strategic, operational, and tactical. It makes no sense for NATO headquarters to do unit training while nations do the operational training. It must be the other way around. NATO headquarters should concentrate on leadership training. They should do joint staff training, while individual nations should do training on the lower levels and within the services and functional areas.

Another issue relates to the concepts of "jointness" and "combined." Generals and staff officers have to learn to orchestrate the three services, special forces, psychological and information operations movement, and logistics in a multinational environment. That is an area in which all nations have problems—especially training generals and staff officers. With sufficient language skills, Russian general and staff officers will be able to add value to the headquarters, with their professional skills, thus creating a "two-way" education scheme. All participating nations can support these efforts, by hosting milestones of the program: seminars and workshops, as well as exercises.

In sum, after 2006, Russian officers should be able to join PFP exercises at the operational level. And 2010 should be the deadline for Russian Forces—Generals and staff officers as well as selected troops—to reach NATO/PFP standards for NATO-led CJTF joint and combined non-Article 5 operations.

Prospects for Elaboration of Joint Doctrines of Peacemaking Activities of Russia and NATO: Russia's Possible Role in NATO Rapid Reaction Forces

U. V. Morozov

Russian Cooperation with European Organizations and Alliances in Peacemaking in Eurasia

The Russian Federation considers peacemaking within the Commonwealth of Independent States (CIS) to be the most important element of national security. In the post-Soviet era, the responsibility for peacemaking operations has fallen primarily to the federation and its military forces. Participation from other CIS countries is often limited to declarations (e.g., in Tajikistan).

The best example of this is peacemaking operation conducted under the aegis of CIS in the Georgia-Abkhazia conflict zone, for which only Russia supplied peacemaking forces. Russia's independent peacemaking activities (in Southern Ossetia and Pridnestrovye) held back the spread of fighting in the former Soviet areas and dissuaded the conflicting parties from returning to military activities. The operations are partly financed through the Russian budget, with irregular contributions from some other CIS countries and parties that had been involved in conflicts.

Given that the CIS countries have such an attitude toward real peacemaking and the proximity of possible Eurasian conflicts, Russia has found it necessary to conduct operations, independent of CIS, to settle conflicts together with other international institutions, including NATO. It is also considered possible to supplement Russia's military participation in operations within the CIS framework through preventive, economical, and humanitarian measures. It is also expedient to introduce structural changes in the existing guarantees of keeping peace and stability in Eurasia using the common peacemaking mechanism.

Practice shows that, unless certain practical steps are taken in joint peacemaking, Russia's independent attempts to ensure regional security will not be efficient enough. Moreover, CIS, as a regional organization, does not want to conduct its own peacemaking activities alone. The Commonwealth is thus in favor of wide participation of the UN, OSCE, and other international organizations in settling conflicts on CIS territory because these conflicts undermine not only regional but also global security. Countries whose conflicts are in a latent or "frozen" state are interested in settling them with participation of Western security structures.

One possible scenario for improving the process of settling conflicts in the post-Soviet era is the possible transformation of current CIS and UN/OSCE operations into integrated, multiaspect operations under the aegis of a global or regional organization with wide participation of the military, police, and civil personnel of the Russian states and of regional organizations and alliances. Shifting the focus from separating parties in conflict to peacemaking will make it possible to use the potential of these organizations to take more efficient measures to ensure the organized return of refugees and deported persons and the rehabilitation of regional economies.

Despite the different approaches Russia and organizations and alliances take to organizing and implementing peacemaking operations, their cooperation in the field of peacemaking has the prospect of becoming one of the cornerstones of peace and safety in Eurasia. However, the many problems on this path may impede the joint efforts of the regional structures and alliances to ensure peace and safety. In general, these problems can be categorized as questions that these organizations and alliances must answer in the near future:

- Would countries having domestic conflicts want the interference of external forces? How should the opinions of de facto, though unrecognized, states that have appeared as some states have dissolved (Abkhazia, Nagomy Karabakh) be addressed?
- Under what organization's aegis can joint peacemaking actions be conducted, for example, in the formerly Soviet areas? Will western European countries want to participate in such operations under the aegis of the CIS Collective Security Treaty Organization (CIS/CSTO)?
- Who will plan joint operations, and how will their procurement and financing be done? What will the operation direction and monitoring system be?
- And, finally, the main issue: Are Western organizations willing, in practice, to cooperate in this field, undertaking peacemaking responsibility jointly with Russia in the common geopolitical areas?

Answers to the above questions will be required to form a real mechanism of peacekeeping cooperation between OSCE and EC and between NATO and CIS, when it is possible to join (or redistribute) their effort.

Despite the complexity of resolving these questions, those who support integrated peacemaking have argued that it is objectively necessary to combine the efforts of organizations and alliances to stabilize the situation in the common geopolitical area.

1. The members of these organizations and alliances are equally interested in peace and stability, not only in their own countries and their near surroundings but also regionally and globally (in particular, this is indicated by the legislative acts that guide the member countries).[1]
2. At the beginning of the 21st century, regional organizations and alliances have encountered threats and dangers that exclude the use of traditional military forces and methods. At the same time, it was necessary in some situations to use military force to stop the military operations of conflicting parties (operations to enforce peace in the Balkans).
3. These organizations and alliances not only function under normative legislative acts but also have corresponding mechanisms for realizing them (in the West, this is the multina-

---

[1] The practical solution of related problems in the framework of the North Atlantic Alliance should have ensured the "multinational operational force" (MOF) concept, originally proposed to the NATO Council of Ministers by U.S. Defense Secretary L. Aspin in Travemuend (October 1993) and approved at the Brussels summit of leaders of Alliance states and governments in January 1994. The concept envisioned formation of mobile multifunctional force units (operational force), uniting formations of all types of forces, and the joint participation of national armed forces of the NATO members, primarily in response to crises. The purpose of the MOF was to create a response force of less strength than the two other components of OBC NATO (main defense force and strengthening force) but that would include the forces most ready for action and the best equipped—15 percent of NATO military brigades, 17 percent of aircraft, and 40 percent of ships.

tional NRF and EC response force now being established; in CIS these are the collective peacemaking forces and CSTO rapid deployment forces).[2]

4. At the regional level, both the NATO and CIS countries have some experience both with conducting operations and with joint operations (in the course of IFOR, SFOR, KFOR operations on Balkans).[3]

5. The region of the former Soviet Union is of the great geopolitical interest to western European countries—as a bridge connecting West and East, as a potential market, as a supplier of energy resources, etc. The main thing, perhaps, is that instability in formerly Soviet areas directly affects the national interests of western Europe.

6. It is of benefit to Russia, both from the political (legitimization of Russian peacemaking at the international level) and economic (reduction of the cost burden) points of view, to use other regional mechanisms (besides CIS) for postconflict settlement in Eurasia.

Thus, the above facts serve as an argument in favor of profound cooperation in joint peacemaking.

Directions of Cooperation for Russia and NATO in Joint Peacemaking

Establishing a new system of relationships in peacemaking is a matter of common interest for all Eurasian countries. So, on July 4, 2003, the Russia-NATO Council (RNC) meeting at the Foreign Affairs Minister level unanimously acknowledged that, for the last year, it had managed to "do significant work aimed at the welfare of all Euro-Atlantic Region countries. Political modeling of potential peacemaking RNC operations approved by the RNC has a serious future."

This led to the following prospective model for the cooperation of the regional structures and alliances in peacemaking.

Peacemaking forces of NATO and Russia (CIS/CSTO) will be able to act jointly to establish and maintain peace in the common geopolitical area. Additional use of military force is possible (by UN mandate) to enforce the peace. OSCE and EC will be able to concentrate on preventive actions, postconflict settlement, and restoration of peace in cooperation with other organizations and countries.

The joint efforts of peacemaking forces (PF) in the Balkans, in which contingents from NATO, Russian, and other countries participated, suggest the following as possible main directions for future peacemaking cooperation: joint monitoring of military and political developments in potential conflict-generating regions in Eurasia; using the nations' collective influence on the conflicting parties, first through diplomacy and then, in emergencies, via military means to ensure peace and stability; jointly supporting those among the former

---

[2] Currently, the NATO council makes the political decision to conduct a peacemaking operation, at the request of UN or OSCE. Since 1999, conducting peace enforcement operations is envisaged (without a UN mandate) as being outside the Alliance's area of responsibility. Three types of operations are considered acceptable: acting independently, acting as the main body of a coalition of countries, or acting as a "subcontractor" for UN operations. The Alliance has already used military force to achieve operational objectives in the Gulf (during Operations Desert Storm and Desert Fox), in the Balkans (Operations Allied Force and United Guard), and in Afghanistan.

[3] NATO is currently conducting four operations: NATO Stabilization Forces (commenced in December 1999), NATO Kosovo Forces (June 1999), Task Forces "Harvest" (June 1999), Task Forces "Fox" (September 2001) in Macedonia. Operations are mainly financed independently, with the proportional contributions from practically all Alliance members.

conflicting parties who aspire to prevent continuation of the military conflict; developing cooperation between the PF's military and civil elements at the various levels and phases of joint operation; and improving the direction of training for joint peacemaking contingents.

The effectiveness of joint international control over and direction of the situation in a potential conflict-generating region depends on the *multilevel interstate military and political situation monitoring system in the common geopolitical area*. Obviously, such a system would be based on unified organization and methodical principles, and its functional structure would integrate the information, analytical, and technical capabilities to acquire information of a variety of national origins.

Conflict control will be an important part of stabilizing the situation in a region. A substantial part of conflict control in the joint actions could consist of assessing preconditions to forecast potential conflict, possibly settling them in advance; identifying all possible ways to prevent and deescalate conflicts; and identifying algorithms for preventive responses at different conflict phases. At the initial phase of escalation, information, psychological, political, and economic preventive measures could be the most effective. Among the military means are demonstration of force and of the resolution to use it and preventive deployment of PF in the conflict-generating area.

A Potential Mechanism for Realizing Cooperation

Obviously, with more active and even routine use of NATO as an instrument for peacemaking in Europe and adjacent regions, it would be expedient to strengthen the normative and legislative bases for nonmilitary operations and the means of implementation. This would enable more complete use of the crisis response potential of the Alliance jointly with Russia in Eurasian.

The Path to Joint Peacemaking

To implement the directions suggested above for joint peacemaking,, it seems expedient to resolve a complex set of issues step by step. The main steps would be for Russia and NATO, and EC and CIS to enter into corresponding international peacemaking memorandums (treaties): for international (regional) and national normative and legislative bases for peacemaking to be harmonized; for integrated regional situation monitoring and peacemaking force control to be set up; and for principles of procurement and financing of joint operations to be specified.

The first step on the way to the joint peacemaking after entering into the corresponding treaties and agreements mentioned above should be to develop a project on doctrines (concepts) of peacemaking activities in Eurasian, which would involve international experts from the UN, OSCE, CIS, NATO, and EC. The second step would then be international adoption of this doctrine, along with formal national legislative consideration. It may be possible to unify and revise the related national normative and legislative bases while the doctrine is being prepared.[4]

---

[4] Against a background of practical NATO participation in conflict settlement within the former Yugoslavia at the beginning of the 1990s, some attempts were made to formulate a specific Alliance "peacemaking" doctrine. The first document that the NATO Military Committee adopted on this subject, in August 1993, reflected the American thesis that there was no distinction in principle between "peacekeeping" and "forced appeasement." Peacekeeping forces were required to be able

The third step would be setting up (or improving) an integrated system of monitoring and joint analysis of the situational developments within the area of common interest to identify potential conflict zones on a regional scale. This could include linking national technical means together to control a regional situation and uniting (international) analytical bodies. In parallel, it would be expedient to specify (or develop) a system for taking joint, practical preventive actions[5] in potential conflict-generating areas to prevent disputes and conflicts leading to armed conflict. Such measures seem to envisage taking joint information and psychological, political, and economic measures against the conflict initiators.

The last step, and one of the most important, will be improving the decisionmaking mechanism for carrying out joint peacemaking operations by ensuring that all concerned national authorities participate equally in collective planning. In parallel, it would be expedient to conduct a complex series of measures to set up an integrated system for PF military and civil component control at the regional and subregional levels.[6]

Investments in Joint Peacemaking

Investments in PF preparation and joint application are also complex and will therefore likewise require a step-by-step approach. This is probably the most difficult task, but it is critical for peacemaking effectiveness. The difficulty can, however, be overcome through political will, the parties' desire, and their relative economic contributions to joint peacemaking.

Military Jurisdiction

Finally, it would be reasonable to specify what falls under the jurisdiction of the military. The first step here would be formulating the key parameters of a universal (modular) execution plans for each category of tasks for both the military and civil aspects of peacemaking. This plan could be supplemented and made more specific, depending on the particular conditions for a forthcoming operation. It seems very important to specify the terminology and staff procedures for planning and conducting joint operations and to ensure the organizational and technical compatibility of the reconnaissance and the troop and weapon control systems. As the experience of the multinational force in the Balkans has shown, it is necessary to develop coordinated approaches to the use of military force and recommendations for its use in advance. Because the levels of training vary among national peacemaking contingents, unified standards are necessary as is carrying out basic and special training for national PF and establishing common regional training centers (using existing national centers) for joint training of PF units and subunits. To assess the effectiveness of the operational plan, it would be helpful to develop a mechanism for estimating the effectiveness of PF use during an

---

to "operationally transfer from one form of peacekeeping activity to another," which depended on the "readiness to resort to the escalation of military operations to achieve military objectives." Subsequent NATO documentation has been characterized by drawing closer to the American approach to peacemaking.

[5] It should be noted that using the strategic concept is a particularly clear example of the Alliance's problems in the parrying threats related to local and regional ethnic and political conflicts. So, NATO strategic documents obviously underestimate the specifics of nonmilitary operations as the basis for the "crisis response."

[6] In the framework of the integrated NATO military structure, MOF operations required a new command system, built on the principle of "detachment but not separation." The idea is to use staff from a regional NATO command to set up the operational headquarters for a particular operation, which would then be strengthened by adding adequate modules ("grouping blocks"). This would have ensured the maximum use of resources of regional NATO commands and, accordingly, significant savings in cost and time (a matter of great significance in terms of crisis response). It was that this plan would be extended to the whole area of staffing the NATO peacemaking contingents, including cooperation with WEC and participation of member countries in the Partnership for Peace (PFP) program.

operation. This mechanism would be based on a system of indices defining the completeness of fulfillment of tasks for various operational phases. To facilitate this provision, a united analytical group should be established so that the peacemaking forces can jointly collect, summarize, and analyze data on the preparation and conduct of the operation. This group should have unified methods for estimating effectiveness.

Terminology

Obviously, as peacemaking theory develops further, it would also be reasonable to set up a unified glossary of terms and concepts for this discipline. Rather wide differences of opinion exist at the international, global, regional and national levels about definitions of various peacemaking actions. Each structure involved in peacemaking interprets these actions in its own way, which makes the practical interoperability of states, organizations, and alliances problematic.

Potential Russian Participation in the NATO Response Force

Realistically, it is reasonable for Russia to consider cooperation with NATO important, in the interests of maintaining the security and stability of the continent. The necessary base for this purpose was established in two documents: the "Founding Act on Mutual Relations, Cooperation and Security Between NATO and The Russian Federation" and "NATO-Russia Relations: A New Quality." [7]

It is quite natural that the intensity of cooperation with the North-Atlantic Alliance will greatly depend on NATO's compliance with the key provisions of these documents, most notably not using violence and threats of violence and not distributing general armed forces, nuclear weapons, and means of their transportation inside the territories of new group members. Rich and constructive cooperation between Russia and NATO is possible only with due consideration for interests of the parties and with the mandatory fulfillment of mutually undertaken obligations.

Russia and NATO have common ideas about the character of threats and the wide opportunities for developing cooperation mechanisms. Thus, setting up new relationship is in the interests of both NATO and Russia, which favor maintaining the security of all Eurasian countries. Taking these common views and moving toward effective joint actions will require concentrated efforts on several interconnected areas and tasks. [8]

Because of the need to fulfill mutual obligations, Russia-NATO cooperation will require closer partnership than ever before, starting with wider and more multilateral consultations on the key problems. As the relationship develops, this could lead to greater interoperability. At that point, Russia, together with other concerned non-NATO parties, would take a more and more active part in the decisionmaking process and in NATO actions (excluding obligations under Article 5 of Washington Treaty). At some stage, Russian coop-

---

[7] See Founding Act on Mutual Relations, Cooperation and Security Between NATO and The Russian Federation, Paris, May 1997, and Heads of State and Government of NATO Member States and the Russian Federation, "NATO-Russia Relations: A New Quality," Rome, May 25, 2002.

[8] See Council for the Foreign and Defence Policy, *New Challenges to Security and Russia*, 2002. Online at www.sv0p.ru.

eration in NATO may become necessary for ensuring overall security, both inside and outside Europe.[9]

The first step toward closer partnership might be a bilateral Russia-U.S. treaty on safeguarding mutual security (but not the mutual defense), together with a series of similar agreements between Russia and other NATO members. Such agreements could actually legitimate the existing state of affairs and would recognize the necessity for developing bilateral relations in the area of security. The result would resemble a formal alliance.

Russia and NATO could also cooperate to develop solutions for the following:

- establishing and maintaining stable relations while maintaining adequate levels of confidence and transparency, which will determine the future state of Russia-NATO relations in the framework of the Russia-NATO Council
- implementing the principle of joint responsibility for jointly taken decisions in the agreed areas and on the basis of consensus
- developing agendas determining joint tasks within the common European area
- applying the benefits resulting from such Russia-NATO cooperation to activities involving other organizations and institutions, such as EC, OSCE, UN, as well as within bilateral relations
- using the above measures as a reliable basis for enhancing the ability of Russia and NATO to jointly counteract threats outside Europe.

Focusing Russia-NATO Council work in this direction would help mitigate differences related to NATO expansion through development of a comprehensive model for ensuring European and Eurasian security. It follows from this that it will be necessary to set up additional mechanisms for collective decisionmaking, including Russian participation. Within the Council framework, it would obviously be expedient to discuss issues related to military doctrines and plans, including jointly establishing principles for the use of force, cooperation in counterterrorism, and joint peacemaking and peacekeeping actions.

The following can be included in the direction of cooperation in the area of joint peacemaking:

- Russia could be included in the NATO exercise planning process and could participate in such exercises. NATO could likewise participate in Russian exercise planning and exercises. It may be necessary to establish a political group to assist in the exercise planning to prevent adoption of potentially provocative exercise scenarios.
- Russia could become involved in developing concepts for using the common joint operational and task force (CJTF), thus becoming party to agreements on objectives, activities, concepts for using these forces use, and their requirements (a military structure, control, a direction and reconnaissance system, etc.).
- It is also possible to establish a joint Russia-NATO brigade (as envisioned during the Clinton administration). The main task of this brigade could, for example, be participation in counterterrorism. The brigade might also have peacemaking status, with its capabilities available for developing united peacemaking doctrine.
- A structure needs to be developed for joint and coordinated peacemaking operations and identification of peacemaking activity planning, management, procurement, and

---

[9] See ISKRAN, "Transition to the New Relationship Between Russia and the West," April 12, 2002.

support conditions, as well as for planning the ability to provide "heightened fighting trim forces" for quick response, if required. The first such document draft has been already developed by the Russia-NATO Council.[10]

- A formal agreement needs to be made about the procedures for conducting joint or coordinated operations on the basis of international law.

- Joint training needs to be arranged for those who will participate in peacemaking operations. This should involve other units from PFP countries as much as possible, so that they can participate in training for joint united operations and tactics. This would allow European countries that are not NATO members to join the process.

- A financing system needs to be developed that takes into account the funds members can contribute to finance the joint activity (e.g., for training the staff and conducting exercises).

- It would be expedient to coordinate the development of the Russia-NATO relationship (including the activities of the Russia-NATO Council) in parallel with relationships among NATO, the European community, and Russia. This will help achieve the common goal of nearly complete integration of Russia into the Western institutions.

The extension of cooperation in Central Asia is also possible, including support of peace, conflict settlement, and emergency response. The specific areas of cooperation, including not only the Central Asia but also other unstable or potentially dangerous regions of the world, need to be identified.

Conclusions

The discussion above leads to the following conclusions:

1. It would be expedient to increase efforts to improve the legal mechanisms for decision-making on conducting peacekeeping operations, including developing the legal basis for using armed forces in peacekeeping and restoration operations. One promising direction for the work may be entering into special normative and legal acts related to joint peacekeeping in Eurasia (doctrines, memorandums, conventions). The objective would be to regulate the actions of armed forces in peacekeeping operations, which in turn would be the logical continuation of the standard formation process, which began with the Hague Regulation of 1899 and developed through later conventions, treaties, and agreements.

2. For the sake of continental security and stability, cooperation with *NATO* is expedient for Russia. This cooperation can be channeled into establishing and maintaining stable relations in ways that maintain an adequate level of trust and transparency; establishing the principle of common liability for jointly made decisions in areas of mutual interest, based on consensus; applying the benefits of Russia-NATO interoperability to the activities of other organizations and institutions, such as EC, OSCE, UN, as well as in the bilateral relationship; and using all these measures to enhance the ability of Russia and NATO to jointly counteract threats outside Europe.

---

[10] See NRC, "Political Aspects of a Generic Concept of Joint NATO-Russia Peacekeeping Operations," Annex 1, 2002

3. It may be possible to improve the conflict settlement process in formerly Soviet areas by transforming current operations into complex, multiaspect operations under the aegis of a global or regional organization, with the wide participation from military, police, and civil staff of the states and regional organizations and alliances. Shifting the emphasis in such operations from separating the parties to building peace would allow such organizations to take more effective measures to ensure the organized return of refugees and displaced persons and the economical rehabilitation of the regions. Even though Russia and these organizations and alliances arrange and conduct peacemaking operations differently, the cooperation among RF, CIS/CSTO, OSCE, NATO, and EC in peacemaking could well become one of the cornerstones of peace and security in Eurasia.

4. If the joint peacemaking model obtains, the peacemaking forces of EC, NATO, and Russia (CIS/CSTO) could conduct operations and actions for establishing and keeping the peace in areas of common geopolitical interest. Additional use of military force (by UN mandate) for peace enforcement operations is also possible. OSCE could concentrate on preventive diplomacy and postconflict settlement and peace restoration in cooperation with other organizations and countries.

5. The following are some key directions for future joint peacemaking cooperation: jointly monitoring military and political situations in conflict-generating regions of Eurasia; exerting collective influence on the parties in conflict, starting with diplomatic efforts and, in an emergency, using military means to provide peace and stability; actively joint supporting those among the former conflicting parties who want to prevent military conflict from continuing; developing cooperation between military and civil PF components at the various levels and phases of joint operations; and improving joint peacemaking contingent training.

6. Implementing such a joint peacemaking activity requires addressing certain issues in sequence. Key among these are international treaties for peacemaking among Russia, OSCE, NATO, EC and CIS; harmonizing international, regional, and national norms and law related to peacemaking; setting up integrated systems for regional situation monitoring and controlling peacemaking forces; and specifying procurement and financing principles for joint operations. Once the treaties and agreements have been entered into, the next step would be for a body of international (UN, OSCE, CIS, NATO, and EC) experts to prepare a formal doctrine for peacemaking activities in Eurasia.

7. Later on, an integrated system for monitoring and joint analysis of developments may be established (or improved) to identify potential regional conflict zones. This system could include national technical and regional situation control facilities linked with each other and to international analytical bodies. The tasks for this include formulating the parameters of a universal (modular) execution plan covering the military and civil aspects of peacemaking for each category of tasks; elaboration of unified basing and special training standards for national PFs and establishing common regional training centers for joint training; and developing a means of estimating the effectiveness of forces during an operation.

8. With the rapid evolution of regional peacemaking in recent years, such concepts as "coalition peacemaking," "police operations," and "humanitarian intervention" have become popular. Some have taken serious exception to how these can be realized, to say nothing of the relevant principles and legal mechanisms, and the subject needs serious theoretical

study. The frameworks of the regional organizations lack details on and, in some cases, simply lack unified approaches to peacemaking (particularly in peace enforcement). This interferes with development of an effective model for the regional security system, gives rise to dangerous precedents of uncontrolled interference, and generates a certain amount of antagonism in relations between countries. The need to codify international peacemaking, in all its diversity, is urgent.

9. The issue of lawfulness of the use of military force use to settle armed conflicts has become more and more topical. In the overwhelming majority of peacemaking operations over the past decade, peacemakers' use of military force has steadily escalated. At the same time, any use of force should be justified and selective, depending on the specific conditions and phase of conflict, and its character; scale; and, most of all, lawfulness should be carefully balanced. The full-scale use of military force to enforce peace among parties, in the framework of the UN Charter, Chapter VII, will obviously continue to be the last resort for peace and restoration of security and must be used only when all other means of influence have been exhausted. The military force must be used in strict compliance with the spirit and letter of the UNO Charter.

Outlook for Cooperation Between the Defense and Industrial Complexes of Russia and the NATO Countries

Vladimir Rubanov

Russia in the Modern World

Nowadays the viewpoint is popular that Russia today is not only no longer a superpower or even a great world power but is only an "influential regional power." However, when considering its nuclear potential, which is still the main parameter of military power, and its territory, natural and power resources, generation of power of various kinds, and fundamental sciences, Russia is still a superstate. The country has a lot of the components of the real sovereignty, which makes possible its active intervention in global processes. But the preservation and strengthening of this status depend on our ability to create a modern economy based on the use and development of "human capital," and this factor is becoming more and more important every day, as never before.

The result of the demilitarization of the Russian economy was a dramatic decrease in the social status of thousands of people having unique and dangerous knowledge, which under certain circumstances can threaten the safety of many countries. Today, as the international community faces the threat of terrorism, this problem takes on worldwide significance and demands that NATO countries take part in the destiny of Russia's defense and industrial complex.

The State of the Russian Defense-Industrial Complex and Prospects for Its Development

Assessment of the Results Gained in Reforming the Defense-Industrial Complex

The end of the "cold war" and reduction of the world armament market made it necessary to reform the defense-industrial complexes of the main opposed centers: the USA and Russia. The Russian government was not engaged in reforming the defense-industrial complex for over ten years. In particular, E. Gaidar's government considered the defense-industrial complex to be a monster that should be destroyed in general. Hence, in those years, the scope of government contractual defense work decreased dramatically from that of the 1980s. Such a policy has resulted in catastrophic consequences for the majority of the enterprises of the defense-industrial complex, and the average level of loading of the defense-industrial complex enterprises now is a maximum of 22 percent or lower. Deterioration of fixed capital stocks of the defense-industrial complex is about 50 percent, with machinery and equipment up to 70 percent, and 95 percent among them have not been updated for a decade. The defense-industrial complex has ceased to develop new engineering almost completely.

The result of that insufficiently considered restructuring was a break of engineering ties and chains that had existed for years between the designers and factories; consequently, the underused and overexcessive structure of the defense-industrial complex had to be financed from a government budget, which was not an effective and rational solution. The actual situation with government contractual work in the Russian defense sector can be expressed as a ratio of 15:85. In the given ratio, 15 percent is for government contractual defense work, and 85 percent is the volume of monetary means to be sought by any defense enterprise from other sources. This situation was officially recognized by the President of the Russian Federation, V. V. Putin, and the order he issued for the defense-industrial complex was as follows: Accelerate integration, starting from the bottom; do not apply to the government for money; and try to find foreign partners and investors.

Therefore, the highest leader of Russia actually recognized, although implicitly, that Russia had basically lost its ability to create independently modern military engineering simultaneously in various directions, and this ability is restricted for financial, technological, and scientific reasons.

But even in this situation of unreasonable economic policy and despite the deformed structure, the defense-industrial complex retains and applies its high potential and keeps an essential segment of the world weapon market. This allows some three to four dozen Russian defense enterprises to remain on their feet, although it impedes their development of new military techniques and financing of large-scale research and development work.

Problems with the Interaction Between the Civil and Military Sectors of the Russian Economy

The defense-industrial complex is probably the sole group that could allow Russia to enter WTO and to integrate into the global economy.

The influence of the defense-industrial complex on the national economy is huge and has deep historical roots. The industrialization carried out in the first half of the last century resulted in total subordination of all industry to military interests and a uniform mobilization plan. In Russia, not only a military and industry complex was created, but also a militarized economy was established in general. Such a system is opposite to the American approach, which is based on a resolute unacceptability of a specialized military and defense complex in general on solving mobilization tasks by supporting high-tech civil industry.

Problems and difficulties of dismantling and modernizing a structurally militarized economy were ignored by Russian reformers, and their inability to realize this and restructure the mobilization and preparedness activity system inherited from the USSR was one their largest mistakes. Under conditions of poor financing, all troubles, problems, and difficulties relative to support all the mobilization-target facilities overloaded the defense enterprises and became one among many factors promoting their economic decline.

The problem can be solved in such a way as to make the enterprises that specialized in output of traditional highly specialized armament (artillery and rifles, ammunition, and explosive substances) state enterprises with fill-in budget financing from the Ministry of Defense. As for high-end technology defense enterprises that can manufacture dual-purpose products, it seems reasonable to allow them to be incorporated with issuing shares, and manufacturing of military products and maintenance of mobilization facilities for these enterprises can be performed within the framework of government contractual defense work on a competitive basis.

There is distorted information about high profitability of the existing weapon systems as Russian export articles. As a matter of fact, today this profitability is due to the zero cost of equipment and the well-skilled labor forces inherited from the USSR and to the fact that the cost of design development work is not included in production cost. However, when applying a new system to manufacture new products, the situation changes, and financial resources will be required to pay for new equipment and for preparation and training of new labor forces that will make Russian armament systems more expensive than American ones. But these problems were not reflected in documentation dealing with reformation and development of the defense-industrial complex.

Because of the above, diversifying the defense-industrial complex enterprises seems to be one possible strategy allowing their economic survival and retention of their technological abilities to output high-tech defense products. Hence, many manufacturers of military materials tend to produce civilian analogs. But this could solve the problem of preservation of the defense-industrial complex, with 15 percent loading of enterprises for purely defense tasks under regular government financing, and loading with the remaining 85 percent for dual-purpose application technology, on the grounds of the principles of economic feasibility and competition.

The Programs of Conversion and of Dual-Purpose Technology

It hardly can be promising for an economy when one tries to force military design offices and military factories to compete in the segments that have been developed for a long time by civil companies. To determine and establish a new market for which one can "arrange" technologies developed in the military and defense complex, one needs a business initiative that is not an inherent feature of all traditional defense enterprises. Conversion of missiles carriers reduced under Strategic Defense Initiative agreements, and their use on the world market of space services, is a good illustration of the above statement and is also an example of successful application of dual-purpose technologies. For successful conversion, it is necessary to combine "know-how" with capacity for commercialization and ability to develop a new market suitable for the new service, in a three-dimensional space including "technological novelty," "market potential," and "business activity." All these directions are equally important. The complexity of the innovation process is that all its integral parts are born and developed simultaneously. Conversion represents a version of the innovation process in which the know-how required for commercialization is of military origin.

To achieve good economic results, the state organization supervising military technologies should decide for itself which parts will remain purely military and which could be converted to commercial uses. Emphasis on the term "dual-purpose technology" makes the situation ambiguous, as is taking a business initiative when unsolved problems remain relative to state secrets and intellectual property rights.

Manufacturing of high-tech production for civilian use while still having the ability to fulfill government contractual defense work allows enterprises not only to be economically independent in the situation of limited demand for defense and military products but also to keep engineering skills vital and ready to work while developing the skills and experience an independent business needs to function in a complex competitive environment.

Legislative Regulations and Organization of Functioning of the Russian Defense-Industrial Complex

The Russian defense-industrial complex will exist and develop strictly within legislative and legal limits. At present, the legislative basis is formed by federal laws, specifically the following, among others:

- About Government Contractual Defense Work
- About Financing of Government Contractual Defense Work for Strategic Nuclear Forces of the Russian Federation
- About Licensing of Some Types of Business
- About Export Control
- About State Regulation of Export Trading
- About Military and Technical Cooperation between the Russian Federation and Foreign States.

Approximately 15 administration bills that the Russian government determined to be priorities for the defense-industrial complex are under consideration by the State Duma (Russian parliament).

The present stage of defense-industrial complex reform is being carried out in keeping with decree No. 1768 of 23 October 2000, "About the Measures to Be Taken for Concentration and Rationalization of the Defense Industry in the Russian Federation," issued by the President of the Russian Federation. This decree set out the rules for establishing holding companies and privatizing defense enterprises, as well as for governmental participation in the resulting entities. A governmental body wishing to participate in a holding company so created must provide at least 51 percent of the shares of its authorized capital.

Alternative models of integration of the state defense sector of the economy are represented by the Sukhoi company and the NPO Ergomash scientific and industrial association. The former is based on the idea of establishing a new managing company to handle state share-holding and to manage financial funds. The latter proposes gathering together certain enterprises that, for whatever reason (very often, by subjective preference) have gained a position of leadership in the cooperation process.

An important organizational measure in reforming the defense-industrial complex was establishing of a new state agency: the State Committee on government contractual defense work at the Ministry of Defense of the Russian Federation. This solution changed dramatically the established system of distribution of authority between Russian governmental bodies. Thus, authority was redistributed between the government and powerful defense agencies that are directly subordinate to the president of Russia, with concentration of all the resources intended for the defense-industrial complex and balanced placement of government contractual defense work orders. Nominally, the State Committee belongs to the Ministry of Defense, but it is actually directed by the Administration of the President of Russia. There are some organizational preconditions for developing military and industrial policy and management of the defense-industrial complex.

The Russian Defense-Industrial Complex and the NATO Countries on the World Armament Market

World Armament Market

The world market for weapons is predictable and stable enough. According to data provided by the London International Institute of Strategic Studies (IISS), the market has been stagnant since 1987: Its capacity has decreased by a factor of almost 2.5 (in 1987, the amount of sold armament was $78.6 billion; in 2000, this figure was $29.3 billion).

The U.S. share of this reduced armament market increased over the last decade, from 25 percent up to 40–43 percent, and Russia's share decreased from 37 percent to 11–14 percent. The Russian losses were due to the destruction of the former management system for controlling export of military products and the loss of partners as a result of the long search for new ways to manage military and defense cooperation with foreign countries.

At the same time, the Russian system for military and defense cooperation proves the presence of a certain stability and a huge internal (latent) potential, and the military complex started to develop and grow. Russia gained some serious results in the Asian market for weapons—Vietnam, Malaysia, Indonesia. Some reserves were also established in other regional markets. Nowadays, the volume of Russian armament supply meets the actual needs of the country, and 2003 was a record year for Russian sales of armaments on the world market. Earnings have exceeded $5 billion U.S.

The share of aircraft engineering in Russian armament exports is 70 percent. Today, the Russian aircraft industry is surviving basically by exporting military aircraft, primarily to India and China. Export of civilian planes is practically absent, as is the domestic demand for them. Therefore, export prospects for military aircraft are vitally important for the defense-industrial complex and for the advanced technology segment of the Russian economy. Antiaircraft defense and naval forces play essential roles in military export.

The system of military and technical cooperation in Russia, the essential element of which is *Rosoboroneksport*, has basically reached a steady state and has proven its vital capacity. The Committee of the Russian Federation on military and technical cooperation has been established as the chief body of executive authority for military and technical cooperation between Russian and foreign countries.

Russian Problems in Military and Technical Cooperation

Financial plans play an essential role in competition in world armament markets. The financial resources of Russian special exporters and defense enterprises, and of Russia in general, are limited, which impedes large-scale programs rendering defensive services at the same time as it supplies armaments. In contrast, this has always been possible in the United States.

Russia is still behind the world leaders in developing modern maintenance systems for its technology. Russia does not have sufficient resources to provide trade discounts to make its related products (such as armaments), parts, and services attractive, given the existing supplies of armaments, spare parts and services. As a result, markets in CIS countries, former Warsaw treaty countries, and Arabian countries are occupied by Israel, France, and a number of other states.

Not only industrial structures but also design and technology offices need to be restructured. Computerization of these structures is now going on. Implementation of Continuous Acquisition and Life Cycle Support (CALS) principles at every stage of the life cycle of any item, from planning to operation, has become an insistent need. Application of up-to-date information technologies allows one to constrain the price that attends more and more complicated military engineering and allows the Russian defense-industrial complex to take part in international cooperation.

Today, the trend is for the military to play a key role in military export enterprises. However, *Rosoboroneksport* had almost 94 percent of all exports in 2003, proving that, in the work that enterprises and others have performed, military and technical cooperation has been insufficient and ineffective. A lot of work should spent on developing ties with new subjects for military and technical cooperation that have the right to export spare parts for military production purposes and to perform maintenance and repair work.

Improving the quality of products supplied for export and providing after-sale services are extremely important tasks. The problem can be solved by transferring this function from *Rosoboroneksport* to defense-industrial complex enterprises and to special structures and bodies that have the right to conduct foreign economic activities independently. The problem of the quality of the after-sale services for high-performance technologies is difficult to solve because of the decrease in the qualification levels of personnel, the loss of skilled workers, and also the minimal volume of armament sales made to the Russian army. Today, repeat manufacturing is actually absent; as a result, skillfulness and technologies tend to be lost.

A number of Russian defense and industry firms are competing with each other in foreign markets abroad. This tendency is rather undesirable for the export of Russian armaments. It not only destroys the unity of public policy on military and technical cooperation between Russia and foreign countries, it also threatens to upset work for concluding contracts for armaments. Thus, in October 1999, the Ministry of Defense of Greece accused Russia, absolutely fairly, of delivering poor-quality C-300PMU1 antiaircraft and missile systems. Such scandals have attracted a loud international response.

Competition Between the Russian Defense-Industrial Complex and NATO Countries in the World Market

The world armament market is closely connected to world policy, which has resulted in application of unfair competition and restrictive business practices and the use of uneconomic methods to push competitors from certain markets or blocking the participation of Russian enterprises in tenders for supply of military and technical.

For example, a number of countries of the Central and Eastern European countries have intended to improve their armament, such as military aircraft, since the end of the Warsaw treaty period to meet NATO standards. The manufacturers and their European partners have faced strong opposition from the United States. Experts have recognized that the reason for this is a desire to sell secondhand early model F-16s that are not necessary for the American air force. The United States sets a rather low price for such planes, so the prices are close to the dumping level, with the purpose of ousting Russian competitors from the market.

The United States has put nonstop pressure on Russia in connection with Russian-Iranian military and technical cooperation. Political gambling on the tragedy of 11 September 2001, application of double-standards, and the use of doubtful or unproved information have contributed to the obstacles to military and technical cooperation between

Russia and Iran, which is a traditional geopolitical opponent of Washington in the region and has a large armament market.

There has been a tendency to transfer contracts for updating and modernizing Soviet and Russian engineering to third countries, to which the Russian party has a natural negative reaction. Russia has persistently asked Israel to change its current policy of competing for cooperation in upgraded programs in the markets of third countries.

One important event was Russia's sale of fighters to Austria in early 1999, which marked its return to the European market, from which Western countries have tried to exclude it. Until recently, the MiG corporation had been fighting for this market. As a result of persistence shown in this case, some of Austria's neighbors (Hungary, Bulgaria, Slovakia) have chosen to buy Russian MiG fighters despite the active opposition of Western competitors.

Recently, India became a source of intense competition between the United States and Russia, as this region is an economically attractive military market. The United States initiated the main challenge to prospects for sales of Russian military aircraft. The U.S. Joint Strike Fighter has been designed not only for arming or rearming NATO countries (although this was also a purpose) but also for ousting both Russia and Europe from the world market.

Russia thus has had to take a considered approach to military and technical cooperation with the various NATO countries, in each case taking into account the degree of accord as well as the potential conflicts of interest.

Areas and Directions of Cooperation

Aviation

The topic of cooperation in aviation is very broad. The most important dimension is creation of a fifth-generation fighter plane. According to American analysts' forecasts, the world market for fighters, in contrast to that for common armament equipment, will grow and will be $17.1 billion by 2007. During this period, the market will be dominated by the American F-15 and F-16, the French Rafale fighter, and the Russian Su-27 and its modification, the Su-30. In 2004–2005, the situation will gradually start changing in favor of the United States. The United States will be more active in promoting its already-operational fifth-generation heavy fighter, the F-22 Raptor.

But even in these conditions of tough competition, Russia has a good chance of keeping and strengthening its positions in the military aircraft market, provided that it speeds up its development of a fifth-generation fighter. If Americans sell 3,000 F-35s at $50 million each, as planned, the Russian fighter plane would cost $35 to $45 million.

The MiG corporation has many years of practical experience working with foreign partners in joint ventures and in jointly operating and modernizing the delivered aircraft. The largest European concerns, EADS and TALES, and the French company SNECMA are its partners. The company also has considerable experience working with MAPS, a Russian-German enterprise, and has operating technical centers in Malaysia and India. The MiG-AT board was created together with French companies. According to expert assessments, MiG-AT could win 25 percent of the world market for training aircraft. Algeria, India, and Greece are already interested in it. In 2001–2002, MiG won competitions against leading Western companies in Hungary, Bulgaria, and Slovakia for contracts to supply and modernize their fighter plane fleets.

RSK MiG and a German company, STN-Atlas, have created a new flight simulator imitating the compartment of the MiG-29 fighter, which will be a basis for establishing centers for training MiG-29 pilots for eastern European countries. Such centers could appear in other regions, to which Russia has already supplied aircraft of the MiG family. The simulator could be sold to such countries as India, Algeria, and Malaysia.

Cooperation between RSK MiG, the EADS aerospace concern, and the German Branch of the British company Rolls-Royce is developing. According to the signed documents, the European partners will undertake some of the functions of Tu-334 procurement, marketing, and certification to European flight readiness standards.

The situation has prompted Russian and European cooperation in creation of the fifth-generation military airplane, because there is the real threat of their being ousted from the market as the American JSF program becomes available. Our allies, in principle, could be France and Germany. There is no reason to count on the investment in the joint development of the fifth-generation aircraft as an alternative to the JSF. But it is possible to exchange European technologies for Russian experience and utilization of intellectual and human potential.

To date, the Russian party has signed a number of protocols of intentions with a French aviation company, Dassault, and European EADS; a joint working group has been established; and a tender for development of specific systems and units for the new fighter has been announced. According to the starting position, the main suppliers of the components and various systems for the fifth-generation fighter are to be Russian partners.

According to experts, development of this international cooperation should not be excluded, because this is the way international aircraft building has been proceeding in creating models of prospective aircraft equipment; the example is the Eurofighter and joint efforts by some European countries and companies in the realization of the JSF program (the F-35). More than ten countries have announced their participation. The realistic strategy for Russia is to take technologies from the West and money from the East, then to proceed with an open international program.

Rockets and Space

In this field, NPO Ergomash and the Lockheed-Martin company are cooperating closely on Proton rockets and the installation of Russian propulsion in American rockets. RD-180s are manufactured in Khimki, Moscow Region. Combustors are supplied from Samara, and special steel from Cheliabinsk.

Boeing Company is greatly interested in a civilian space partnership with Russia. The range of subjects that the Boeing Moscow Representative Office, where 400 people are employed, has widened. America and Russia have the engineering and technological potential required for cooperation and have already cooperated on the International Space Station and the C-Launch. Boeing knows well how to work with the Russian partners and expresses willingness to jointly develop a unified antimissile defense system, subject to the political decisions of U.S. and Russian leaders.

From the technical point of view, the problem is that the major opportunities for joint activity are in the civil space area, in which there are few income-producing projects.

Air Defense

Russia is the only country in the world manufacturing the whole the range of air defense systems, from extra-short range (Igla complex) to extra-long range (C-400). More new Russian air defense systems are surpassing foreign analogues, both technically and in pricing. Even the new American PAC-3 system is inferior to the existing C-300 models. The performance characteristics of the C-400 system currently being tested will certainly surpass those of the upgraded PAC-3 models. Western experts believe that C-400 will be effective for 20 to 50 years.

Currently, the United States is paying great attention to tactical missile defense and to development of the new Theater High-Altitude Air Defense (THAAD) system, intended to ensure that the first layer of the U.S. antimissile defense will be operational. Nobody presumes that the C-400 will be able to compete with THAAD. Taking into account that it takes 10 to 15 years from the design phase to the series production of an air defense system, it would be reasonable for Russia to proceed with a new system. Development of new air defense systems is also connected with creation of the fifth-generation fighter.

The above developments can be considered as possible areas of cooperation with the concerned NATO countries.

Overcoming Antimissile Defense

After completion of the successive phases of the strategic command and staff training in Plesetsk, President Vladimir Putin announced that Russia will soon have up-to-date strategic missiles that will fly at hypersonic speeds, change trajectory by altitude and course, and strike strategic targets at intercontinental distances. American experts consider these Russian achievements to be an asymmetrical response to the American antimissile challenge and possibly a way to overcome the antimissile defense system being developed in the United States. There are no real analogues for this system abroad, which makes it useful for the entire range of antimissile defense system development and deployment problems.

Armored Equipment Protection Systems

The design mechanical engineering office (Kolomna) has designed the Arena system, which is currently being tested. This system can protect a tank, with a high degree of probability, against destruction by antitank grenades and by guided and nonguided missiles shot from all types of infantry weapons. Arena can spot and destroy any targets flying to the tank.

Equipping a tank with such a system double its chances of survival, at a price increase of only 20 percent. According to one magazine, *Export of Weapons*, worldwide tank sales between 2002 and 2008 will exceed 2,000 pieces. Besides potentially increasing the sales volume for Russian armored machinery, this technology can also be used in other forms of military and engineering cooperation.

Warships and Antiship Weapons

One more type of new weapon that can provide good profits for Russia is the warship. According to data from AMI, an American consulting company, the world market for new warships over the next 15 years is an estimated US$236 billion. Russia has the most advanced technologies for manufacturing torpedo-boat destroyers, corvettes, and nuclear submarines; however, it is difficult to say whether there are any aspects of cooperation with

NATO countries in this area. It seems that economic considerations and the capacity of each country's own facilities will play the determining role.

Russia possesses technologies for creation of antiship missiles, primarily Moskit missiles. This is the only missile in the world with a low altitude speed exceeding 2,800 km/hour. It is absolutely impossible to shake a Moskit flying at an altitude of 3–6 m. It can break through the hull of any ship, then burst inside. Such a blow is able to sink not only a medium-sized ship but even a cruiser. When developing this missile, more than 30 inventions and scientific discoveries were used. Subject to some updates, Moskit can be used as an air-to-surface missile and can be installed in the fifth-generation fighter.

The technological grounds for cooperation between Russia and NATO in this category of weapons are obvious, and its realization lies in the political and economic areas.

Communication and Control Systems

It is obvious to Russian military leaders that it is necessary to establish a complex armed-forces control system that can function in today's world. The goal is to develop such as system by 2016, which means concentrating efforts on establishing an interdisciplinary multi-functional (integrated) control system that is built on the development and use of software and technical means that have been standardized as much as possible and that are compatible, one that minimizes the complexity of control points and the means required for the effective direction of troops and all types of military operations support—provided that the control system's operational and strategic requirements are implicitly met.

A digital integral global information transmission network linking end users in various world regions and providing mutual coordination of the communication systems of the operational and tactic control level is in the process of being built to create a unified NATO communication system. Russia is following a similar path, creating a united telecommunication base for the Russian Armed Forces information structure and a united information space for control and support of effective troop and weapon control information technologies. As the system of military communications is a component of the Russian communication infrastructure, a significant part of military tasks can be completed using the country's United Electrical Communication Network.

The close relationship between civil and military information and communication resources enables us to speak about the broader context of cooperation between Russia and NATO countries in this area, bearing in mind the leadership of the United States and Europe in information technologies. NATO counties' experience and provision of control systems that are compatible with NATO standards ensure the possibility for Russia to take part in NATO peacekeeping operations.

Information Technologies

The role of platforms and the information space in the military systems is changing significantly. Missiles, tanks, and ships are united by information. To win a battle or war today, it is necessary to handle information properly. So information is not less important than aircraft, tanks and ships. Information and its application technologies are becoming a more and more important military resource. The main difference between the fourth- and fifth-generation aircraft is in their onboard systems and in the transfer of the control of fighting systems to virtual space. This very new function is part of the innovation formula for the fifth-generation aircraft. The significant achievements NATO countries have made in information technologies have inspired Russian interest in cooperation to create the new generation of military equipment.

Generally, when identifying aspects of Russian-European cooperation, consultations have been limited to traditional military technologies (aviation, rocket building, etc.), and little attention has been paid to information technologies. At the same time, the world software market is estimated by survey groups as US$120 billion, and the market for armaments and military equipment has recently been fluctuating around US$30 billion.

In information and communication technologies (ICT), Russia has high potential in the form of a great number of highly skilled mathematicians and programmers. This potential is strategically important for today's economy, but, unfortunately, failure to take advantage of it has led to a "brain drain" from Russia and to impractical use of intellectual resources. The high level of Russian specialists' mathematical culture allows organizing production of original software products for the world market directly in Russia.

This problem can be solved by development of offshore programming. Recently, Russia has been assimilating the experience and increasing the offshore programming potential. Specialized companies have been formed in the Russian market: SiBit, Luxoft, Novosoft, Actis, Argussoft, and a number of others adapted to the ICT world market. In addition to software coding, the ICT and high-tech experts consider pattern recognition and image processing, development of languages and programming systems, communication system software development, bioinformatics, hydrodynamics and physical science to be the most promising prospects for Russia. Knowledge in the above areas allows development of programs supporting scientific research, including military application directions.

A joint Russian-American program, Initiatives for Proliferation Prevention, occupies a separate place in this field. LUXOFT and the U.S. Energy Department are performing this program. The program is aimed at the development of nonmilitary applications for defense technologies and establishment of permanent jobs in the civil industries for scientists and engineers of the defense, including nuclear, industries, as well as conditions for specialists using their expertise in nonmilitary commercial projects.

The program is being sponsored by the National Administration for Nuclear Security at the U.S. Energy Department, with assistance of the U.S. Industry Coalition (USIC), a noncommercial association of U.S. companies and universities that acts as a commercial agent of the program and supports the operations of U.S. industry partners on jointly financed projects.

In the framework of the agreement, LUXOFT functions as a center providing professional retraining to computer scientists at a Russian research center, the Kurchatov Institute, the largest nuclear energy research center in the country. LUXOFT specialists teach groups of scientists from this institute, adapting their brilliant expertise to the commercial production of software. Today, LUXOFT's work has exceeded the limits of the project, and the company has become the largest center of offshore programming in Russia, compared to the large companies of the NATO countries, among which Boeing occupies the prominent place.

This Russian offshore programming potential, however, is used quite insufficiently. While the volume of the offshore programming exceeds US$7 billion annually in India, the volume is approximately US$150 million in Russia (as of 2002).

This insufficient usage of the intellectual and human potential and capability for the large-scale organization of the offshore programming is the result of a disastrous lack of management staff and infrastructure for innovation. This can be overcome through Russian-European cooperation and through replenishment of deficient resources. The emphasis should be placed on the Russian potential to create information security technologies comparable to those of the United States. In developing and providing authorization, authentication, and administration (AAA) facilities, an operation related mainly to cryptography technologies, Russia is one of the world leaders.

Establishing alliances between Western industry companies and Russian scientific and technological centers will ensure combination of the reliability of Western companies with the innovativeness of Russian companies, which will serve as a basis for well-thought out sets of complicated products and engineering solutions for the global market.

Special Equipment

Recently, Russia has rushed the export of special weapons. Special elements added noiseless pistols, machine guns, and sniper rifles, as well as Gurza-type pistols with unrivaled accuracy and similar machine guns to their arsenals in the early 1980s. Up to now, these weapons have remain unmatched in their capabilities and engineering solutions by the leading Western companies. Russian enterprises have achieved rather good results in creating information-gathering systems and in supplying technical security for both facilities and wide areas. They have also created an arsenal of equipment and techniques for law enforcement and civil defense.

The main competitors in this market are French, English, German, and Italian companies, which have completely dominated the market in recent times. But now the Russian brand has managed to breach their positions and has developed self-confidence in the Near- and Middle-East. *Rosoboronexport* is the only company that has offered not just products but also its willingness to provide a whole complex of special deployment elements, from supplying weapons and corresponding equipment to assisting the creation of self-contained systems and staff training.

Russian defense and industrial complex enterprises have competitive solutions for special equipment and are ready to carry out R&D work for foreign partners. The question is only how interested the NATO countries will be in Russian developments and provide equal competitive opportunities in their markets.

Problems of Cooperation Between the Russian Defense-Industrial Complex and NATO Countries

State Secrets and Commercial Classified Information

Despite the end of the Cold War, a number of things have limited the possibilities for effective international cooperation: the disastrous economic situation in the Russian defense-industrial complex, massive development of legal ways to collect military and technology information, and legislation on state secrets and applying them to commercial activities. One Russian Federation law, "About State Secrets," was prepared to define what constitutes a state secret. The resulting list fails to mention any particular information but defines concepts, classes, and categories that can be applicable to practically any classified information. In practice, experts establish what are state secrets, which makes the reasons and the grounds for security classification questionable and suggests conclusions about the degree of secrecy of any particular piece of information.

This situation is in conflict with a statement in the Russian Constitution, which says that any information can be considered secret only according to federal law, not expert examination. The difficulty of correctly applying the legislation lies in incorrect views about the nature of state privacy. The legislation is based on the viewpoint that any information, including common public information, can be assessed fairly through official bureaucratic procedures. As a matter of fact, the designation of a state secret is an expression of the subjective will of state officials within the framework of the power and responsibility given to them for protecting national safety. Experts cannot officially define a state secret, but can only offer opinions about the importance of the data and information items for military and other vital national interests. The illogic of the legislation and its primitive application have resulted in a series of scandals in international scientific and technical cooperation.

Designating a great number of scientific and research programs developed by various enterprises within the defense-industrial complex as "closed" and then actually removing from economic circulation limits international cooperation, thus greatly harming the Russian economy.

Another obvious mistake is that, in applying the current legislation about state secrets, Russian bodies and agencies try to establish relationships that should be subject to civil rights. This position has caused an inadmissible delay in passing another law, "About Commercial Classified Information," by placing unreasonable limits and restrictions on commercialization of the achievements of the defense-industrial complex, even though these unprotected technologies have been removed from the military field. A number of foreign companies have taken advantage of the absence of legislative responsibility in Russia for industrial espionage, which has damaged the interests of the Russian defense-industrial complex. Passing the law on commercial classified information would position the subject legally, much as it is in NATO countries.

Protecting Intellectual Property Rights

A matter of great importance for development of the Russian defense-industrial complex involves economic circulation of intellectual property. For this purpose, it is necessary to coordinate the Russian organization and legal basis for manufacturing and the use of valuable knowledge and technological achievement with European standards. Development of a technical audit to provide complex assessment of intellectual resources could play an essential role in increasing the effective use of intellectual potential of Russian advanced technology enterprises, design offices, and research and development institutions, allowing their commercial potential to be capitalized on and assisting their marketing. Studies of experiences in solving similar problems in enterprises in NATO's defense-industrial complex could be valuable for the Russian defense-industrial complex.

The absence of a legislative basis for managing intellectual property rights creates obstacles for Russia in its relations with countries that produce military products under license from Russia and supply them to third countries without our consent and without payment of suitable royalties. At present, a great preparation work is being performed to compile agreements about the protection of intellectual property rights. Such agreements should be signed with Poland, Hungary, the Czech Republic, Romania, Bulgaria, Slovakia, and a number of other countries. Some such agreements have already been prepared and transferred to the government for approval, and some have already been signed with a number of countries.

Russia has signed an agreement on protection of the intellectual property with Israel, among others. Although Israel is not a NATO country, cooperation with it is essential for Russian defense-industrial enterprises for the markets of European members of the North Atlantic Alliance. For example, the modernization of MiG-21 fighters in Romania was followed by a series of crashes, proving that the Russian developer should not be avoided. Israel works basically on modernizing Russian engineering, since correctly managed cooperation with the Russian defense-industrial complex is of principal importance and has good prospects, because the market for modernization is so large.

Russia has also declared its intention to conclude a multilateral agreement with the United States on the protection of intellectual property, which will allow both parties to approach the development and implementation of joint large-scale projects using advanced technologies.

Standards and Technical Rules

Today's Russian armament is standardized but focuses on its own standards. For this reason, some Russian defense-industrial complex customers have been forced to continue using Russian products because possibilities and resources for leaving the old technical basis are limited.

Development in Russia of CALS technologies and adhering to European standards of information and technological provisions for the life cycles of high-tech products are of principal importance for putting forward scientific and technical cooperation in the field of aircraft, antimissile defense, and other advanced technology products.

Prospects for and Organization of Cooperation

Participation of Russian Defense-Industrial Complex Enterprises in NATO Programs

NATO is not uniform and has complex mechanisms. Within the framework of NATO, some differences can be seen between America and Europe on the most important question: force and its efficiency, morals, and desirability. In determining national priorities, assessing threats and challenges, and formulating and implementing external and defense policy, the United States and Europe, as R. Keigan declared, follow different paths. Therefore, the Russia-NATO Council should become and can become the place for European countries to elaborate weighed and balanced solutions, taking into account national interests and conditions of the dominating role of the United States.

Another circumstance limits possibilities for cooperation with NATO countries, as a group. Although NATO supports expansion of military and technical cooperation with Russia, NATO is not able to effect this expansion on its own. So far, therefore, this cooperation has basically been limited to the conceptual level. Work on practical implementation of this cooperation could be organized within the framework of bilateral agreements with some particular NATO countries.

Cooperation with Individual NATO Countries

Until recently, cooperation between the Russian and French defense and industrial complexes was limited to the installation of French parts on Russian weapons that were exported to third countries. Today, for the first time, Russia is joining with France to develop a new type of armament: a pilotless aircraft (BPLA). In France, the developer was Dassault, a developer of Mirage and Rafale fighters. In Russia, a large team of developers will be created, including the Sukhoi, Yakovlev, and Toupolev design offices. Development of the BPLA will require several billion U.S. dollars, of which the Russian share could be considerable. France will profit from the cooperation with Russia because both countries are behind in the development of BPLA aircraft relative to the United States and Israel (both of which use pilotless aircraft effectively in real operations).

The top management of American Boeing corporation has declared its intention to develop new projects in cooperation with Russia. The main idea of these joint projects is to unify all the programs for developing separate flying platforms, as well as all the projects on satellite communication and information. The resulting system decisions could involve Boeing customers in the American government and could attract worldwide attention. Experts consider combining all information flows on all flying platforms to be a positive direction for military and technological advances.

There are some examples of the Russian-American cooperation in particular areas. Russian An-124 cargo aircraft took part in American military campaigns in 2003 because insufficient U.S. aircraft were available. That allowed the Russian side to earn $29 million. However, the technical ability of the Russian cargo aircraft and the economically attractive services can be made null and void by U.S. government policies, which has already been reflected in some reports and speeches by American congressmen.

However, military and technical cooperation with advanced western countries and, most important, with the United States is a rather complex issue. The Cold War is over, but some stereotypes both in Russia and in USA have survived. Thus, it is not rare for American partners to spend all their efforts trying to get some unique samples of Russian military technology. Most often, such activities relate to the intention of finding effective ways to counter the most effective Russian military technologies. When Russian companies propose mutually beneficial cooperation to their American counterparts, the most frequent reaction from the Americans is "polite rejection."

Russian-American cooperation has tended to decrease in a number of projects that seemed promising. For example, in 1992, former Presidents Bill Clinton and Boris Yeltsin sponsored an antimissile defense project, the Russian-American Observation Satellite (RAMOS). This project provided joint development, start-up, and on-orbit operation for two years of a Russian and American experimental satellite for remote sensing of the earth. If necessary, the orbital flight of the satellites could be prolonged to 5 years. The project was planned to put forward to the stage of practical realization to the end of the current decade.

During the initial phase of the program, in 1995–1999, both countries achieved a certain amount of scientific and technical progress. But then the program became a hostage of the international political situation that arose after the United States decided to leave the Antimissile Defense Treaty and establish a national missile defense system. The top Russian political leaders came out against this decision, and after a while, the Pentagon displayed concern about the security of information collected on the RAMOS program and possibility of disclosure of proprietary American space technologies. This apprehension began to affect project financing. In addition, the Antimissile Defense Agency considered that the expected cost for RAMOS through the completion of the project was too high (approximately US$550 million) and that the funds would be better spent on a "purely American" priority, the missile defense program.

In spite of the decision to close RAMOS, American officials state that they intend to cooperate with Russia in missile defense. But the United States' leaving the program indicates that the near-term prospects for Russian-American military and technical cooperation are rather hazy.

The Euroforum IWGA: R&D Work in the Defense Area and Industry Innovations

The International Working Group on R&D Work in the Defense Area and Industry Innovations (IWGA) will be able to help find ways to improve cooperation between the Russian defense-industrial complex and NATO members; this group functions within the framework of "The New Defense Agenda," under the aegis of EC and NATO and with the support of the C. Adenauer Fund. The IWGA comprises representatives of the European Commission, European Community Council, NATO, NATO Parliament Assembly, West-European Armour Group, large military and industry companies, NATO members' Ministries of Defense, northern and southern European countries' missions in NATO, the C. Adenauer Fund in Brussels, major western European mass media, and a number of European research centers. The main conclusion of the IWGA's report is that there is now a technological gap between the EC and the United States, but only a gap in resources. As such projects as Airbus and Arianne demonstrate, properly mobilizing EC resources can produce the same level of technology as that of the United States.

The most interesting discussion at the Brussels IWGA meeting seems to have been that on the fifth-generation strike fighter. In light of U.S. plans to create such an aircraft by 2012, European countries have had to choose between joining the American JSF program, which Great Britain and the Netherlands have already done, or cooperating with other countries, including Russia, to create a competitive model of the strike aircraft within the same period. In the first case, European countries can count on some part of the Pentagon budget, but then they cease to be independent military and industrial powers. In the second case, Europe will have to rely on its own resources but will preserve its ability to compete with the United States in aviation arms markets in the 21st century. The working group members welcomed Russian proposals. Of particular interest was our proposal of cooperation on creation of the fifth-generation strike fighter.

Experts agree, however, that decisionmaking in each European country will be guided more by political considerations than by potential economical benefits and the needs of the world armament market. In this connection, hopes for the European convention on the cooperation between national military-industrial complexes hardly can be considered completely realistic.

At the same time, the activities of the IWGA seem to be useful for establishing defense and industrial cooperation with European NATO members. To proceed in this direction, it would be expedient to hold a special IWGA meeting in one of the Russian regions having many such enterprises (for example, in Nizhny Novgorod).

Political Relations: RUSSIA, NATO, and the European Union

Vitaliy Zhurkin

In spite of the imposing role that NATO plays in military affairs and the EU in economics, the core political relations in European and Euro-Atlantic areas are still thinned not by unions and alliances but by states themselves—members of these unions, alliances, and coalitions. Major developments in the arena of international politics of the last couple of years are vividly confirming this phenomenon or, better to say, tradition.

The most dramatic political event of this couple of years or so (the period after the tremendous tragedy of 11 September 2001) is the conflict and split in the international community over the Iraqi crisis. The political role of NATO and the European Union in relation to this crisis was practically irrelevant. The players were the states with their clearly (or sometimes not so clearly) defined national interests. Their belonging to this or that alliance or union was purely superficial.

Another of the innumerable examples: Political battles that are raging with varied intensity around the European Constitution. It is educative and often amusing to watch from afar how inventive some nation-states, members of the EU, are in protecting their right to national foreign, security, and defense policy from integrationalists—proponents of CFSP and ESDP. The final result of these clashes and maneuvers is the present state of affairs, in which the drive to European security and defense policy, which so energetically started after the Maastricht treaty and in particular after the historic Franco-British Saint Malo summit, is still mostly and unfortunately on paper. All these are not just unconnected examples but reflections of tendencies that are still quite powerful.

It is only natural in such a situation that Russia tends to pay particular attention to bilateral political relations with the United States and major European powers—France, Germany, Great Britain, Italy, and others. To a certain extent, it resembles the power politics of the Cold War bipolar world, which was often called the world of power blocs but in reality constituted the battlefield of major world powers. The Warsaw Pact played quite a rudimentary role in Soviet global policies. On the other hand, in its first serious political encounter with NATO half a century ago, when the Soviet leadership decided to test the Atlantic Alliance by proposing to join it, Moscow approached not NATO but Washington, London, and Paris and was rejected. Other political encounters with NATO were, in reality, along the same lines. In the contemporary world, which in fundamentally different from the Cold War era, we are nevertheless constantly facing contradictions between national policies and aspirations of unions and alliances.

All these reservations are aimed not at diminishing the importance of relations with Euro-Atlantic and European institutions for Russia but at fitting this set of relations into a realistic political context. At the same time, within this context, there exist quite serious and promising prospects, as defined by several rather obvious reasons.

First, in spite of active criticism from various (in particular Russian) quarters, NATO is developing (though slowly) its political dimension and transforming itself from purely military into a politico-military coalition. NATO's role in pacifying contradictions over the Iraqi crisis could be greater but more and more evident. It is reasonable to expect that the political face of NATO will be more and more visible and effective.

There is a lot of disappointment about a rather ineffective development of the political and especially defensive dimension of the European Union. Although major political decisions are taken, the practice of their implementation needs a lot of improvement. But the political will exists, and it provides a basis for expectations for a more promising future.

Finally, Russia itself is clearly committed to developing a political partnership with both NATO and the European Union. It has officially proclaimed this as an integral part of its foreign policy strategy.

Thus, in spite of certain borders imposed by domestic and international realities, political inertia, opposing national interests, there exists quite a wide base for Russia's cooperation with the Western alliances. Even more important is the fact that these borders are not static. They have a wide potential for enlargement. And they do widen in reality when a mutual desire for partnership and cooperation exists. At least developments in post–Cold War history provide encouraging proof of exactly such a turn of events and prevailing tendencies.

While turning to practical problems and prospects of Russia-NATO political relations and cooperation, it is worthwhile to state that these relations have at least two major functions, which may be called internal (or bilateral) and external.

The internal function is aimed at solving political problems and conflicts that arise in relations between Russia and NATO. The long history of attempts to solve, or at least to smooth, maxi- and mini-crises, which developed around NATO's enlargement into the central and eastern Europe and its approach to Russia's borders is just the most glaring example of such problems. Minor crises may arise in other spheres. Conflicts and contradictions are not ruled out in and around CIS or larger area of the former Soviet Union. There are other potential situations that may lead to frictions and discord, in particular because both sides are burdened with rather influential political forces that are always ready to exploit such situations for their own partisan purposes. If the existing Russia-NATO structures are not adequate for performing this internal or bilateral function, new or additional political instruments should be created.

With due attention to problem-solving in Russia-NATO political cooperation, its main drive is embodied in what may be called the external function: partnership aimed at strengthening international peace and security. All nine present foremost areas for military or military-political cooperation are properly outlined in the Rome declaration, "NATO-Russia Relations: A New Quality,"[1] and in the activities of the NATO-Russia Council with its working groups and subcommittees. One may expect more active implementation of the Rome declaration, but the fact is that the joint work is going on.

A lot in this work depends on political will and the desire for political cooperation. Probably, it will be easier to proceed in spheres where NATO and Russia have already

---

[1] See Heads of State and Government of NATO Member States and the Russian Federation, "NATO-Russia Relations: A New Quality," declaration, Rome, Italy, May 2002; online at http://www.nato.int/docu/basictxt/b020528e.htm (as of September 22, 2004).

achieved certain—maybe still quite modest—advances, such as peacekeeping, antiterrorism, and the struggle against proliferation of weapons of mass destruction. In any case, the potential of Russia and NATO to take larger joint political decisions, aimed at strengthening security in Europe and elsewhere, is still being tapped in quite a limited way. There is a good prospect for really serious breakthroughs.

Russia's political relations with the European Union (with the union, not its major members) look rather paradoxical. The EU is clearly the most important economic partner for Russia. So far as political spheres are concerned, it was traditionally taken for granted that Russia prefers the EU as its main partner in the West. There is a series of well-developed joint statements on cooperation in the fields of foreign policy, security, and defense.

But in practical terms, progress is quite modest. Even the necessary precondition—establishment of a Permanent Council for the Russia-EU partnership—was agreed on only at the end of last year. This council still is in a rather amorphous state. Almost all Russia-EU relations continue to be confined to economics. Everything is there—all major successes of the Russia-EU partnership, all major failures, and all major contradictions (such as the latest ones, which arose around the problem of the application of the Partnership and Cooperation agreement to 10 new members of the EU after May 1, 2004.

Thus, improper development of Russia-EU political relations is primarily the result of the inadequate role the political dimension plays in the life of the European Union. It is the irony of history that the founding fathers of the European integration carefully planned the development of the political and defense pillars of the process and organization parallel to the economic integration practically from the very beginning (European Defense Community and European Political Community of the early 1950s). Their plans did not materialize.

The present materialization of the old plans has not developed adequately. The EU itself is developing common foreign policy, security, and defense with a great—successful, but more unsuccessful—effort. It took a long time to finalize the agreement with NATO on using its assets in the EU operations ("Berlin plus"). The disagreements between major EU players, which emerge, disappear, and reemerge periodically, do not help at all. In such conditions, it would be superfluous to expect that Russia-EU political cooperation would develop smoothly and steadily beyond expressions of goodwill and far-reaching but not very practical plans. But at the same time, the goodwill and ambitious plans are there. They need only time to be put into practice. It is necessary simply to work and wait.

The paradox of the Russia-EU situation is formed by the fact that, at the same time, Russian political relations with major members of the EU (and major European members of NATO) are developing swiftly and effectively. The Franco-Russian Council on security cooperation works actively. Its latest ideas are a new permanent Russia-EU mechanism and a joint concept for crisis settlement. The same is true with Germany, Italy, Great Britain, and so-called "old Europe." In a sense Russia is "old Europe" itself. It is quite possible that these networks of political relations and cooperation will finally facilitate more active Russia-EU (and Russia-NATO) political interaction.

There is one sphere on the European or Euro-Atlantic political landscape that has nothing to do with Russia's national interests. It is the set of problems in relations between NATO and the EU. This complicated web of positive and negative tendencies is wrapped in a bundle of official mutual compliments, and Moscow can only watch from afar. If Russia could do anything to solve any of the problems arising between NATO and the EU, it should act. But this is absolutely beyond its abilities. Thus, it is most reasonable to stay aside and suppress any temptation to fish in muddy waters.

In conclusion, it is necessary to say once more that, for Russia, political relations with both NATO and the European Union contain a lot of ambivalence and even uncertainties. But it would be wrong to underestimate or disregard the positive results that have been achieved. They are the foundation for further efforts and progress.